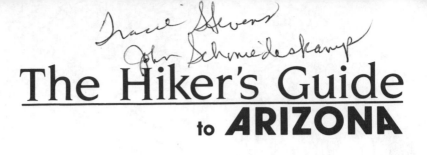

The Hiker's Guide
to **ARIZONA**

Fall 1992

Stewart Aitchison
Bruce Grubbs

The Hiker's Guide
to **ARIZONA**

Stewart Aitchison
Bruce Grubbs

Library of Congress Catalog Card Number: 86-82126

ISBN: 0-934318-93-X

Distribution and Marketing:
Falcon Press, P.O. Box 279, Billings, MT 59103
Editorial and Production:
Falcon Press, P.O. Box 731, Helena, MT 59624

All text, maps, and photos by the authors.
Cover photo by Tom Bean.

FOREWORD

Viewed from a plane, the Arizona landscape looks like a huge relief map. The contours and convolutions of the earth are apparent, with canyons, mountain ranges, mesas, and valleys fitting together. The geologic complexity and immensity of the land is much easier to appreciate. But from a high altitude, the land appears lifeless.

Viewed from a speeding car, the Arizona landscape is constantly changing: from Sonoran desert with its menacing array of spiny plants punctuated by giant saguaro cactus, to gnarly junipers dotting a grass-and-prickly pear plain. The road winds higher, among cool ponderosa pine forests where extinct volcanoes jut skyward. Mysterious twisting canyons, isolated mesa tops, and mountain summits rush by, and only the largest plants are noticeable. Wildlife seems exceptionally sparse—except for frequent and unfortunate road kills.

But traveling on foot, with a backpack filled with necessities and perhaps a few luxuries, we can feel the geology beneath our feet, witness the intricate beauty of a cactus flower, wonder over the life of some ancient cliff dweller, observe the clumsy, comical mating of two desert tortoises, and hear the wild scream of a red-tailed hawk.

Only on foot, close to the land, away from the mechanized world, can we truly appreciate nature and perhaps discover our place in the universe. The trip doesn't have to be an epic two-week-long hike, lugging a sixty-pound backpack on weary shoulders. An afternoon stroll down a flat sandy wash may be sufficient to travel a long way toward understanding and enjoying the natural world.

PREFACE

My favorite place is Sierra Ancha, the wide mountain. In August, when Phoenix heat is no longer bearable, we leave, driving east past Roosevelt Lake, up a rocky track past the forks of Workman Creek, through damp thickets of mountain locust, columbine, and raspberry into the rain forests that cover Aztec Peak. There the road ends. The trail begins.

We spend the mornings on walks through the dense fir and spruce thickets, pausing to gaze across the ramparts of Pueblo Canyon over the honey-colored desert stretching eastward 3,000 feet below. In the afternoon, cumulus clouds build up and explode in a frenzy of lightning, thunder, and sudden cold rain. Evening is a quiet play of light and shadow. As the clouds break and drift away, a pale moon floats up from the pink, receding desert horizon reaching through the twisted branches of old pine.

This is Arizona! Yet, it is also the silence of stone and brilliant light of the inner Grand Canyon, where human significance shrinks to the vanishing point. It is the rainbow of color in the widest vista of the painted desert. It is the spiraling red waves and cobalt light of the Vermilion Cliffs. It is the Gila woodpecker spinning out of her burrow in the saguaro cactus, then pirouetting in space over the sand and gravel reaches of the Sonoran Desert. And, it is the complete circular vision atop the Kachina Wilderness—knowing that this is home to the beings of the Hopi spiritual path.

In Arizona, there is great beauty just one step in any direction. We have four seasons almost any time of year. We have examples of almost every ecosystem type in America. Your awakening to the natural world can come from just one trip to any of the magical places described in this book.

What the authors have done is to make the first and successive trips more feasible. With lucid prose and clear maps, we have before us one of the finest hiking guides for Arizona to date from two of our foremost adventurers. Because many of the places described here are not heavily traveled, the opportunity for new exploration of lesser known places is enhanced. The opportunity for surprise awaits. Only you can take the first step. Now there is no reason to wait another day!

Bruce Babbitt, Governor

TABLE OF CONTENTS

HIKING IN ARIZONA—AN INTRODUCTION

HIKING TECHNIQUES AND ETHICS

MAKING IT A SAFE TRIP

THE HIKES

Southern and western deserts—Superstition Mountains, Santa Catalina Mountains, Rincon Mountains, Santa Rita Mountains, Chiricahua Mountains, Hualapai Mountains.

AFTERWORD

RESOURCES

LOCATION MAP OF HIKES

Use this general map to locate the hikes—by number—in the table of contents. More detailed maps accompany the descriptions of the hikes.

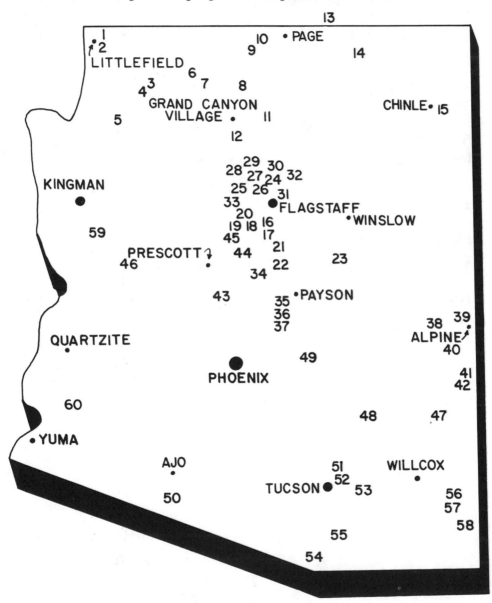

HIKING IN ARIZONA, AN INTRODUCTION

This is obviously a book about hiking in Arizona, but many of you familiar with the state may wonder about some glaring omissions. Where, for example, is a description of the popular Bright Angel Trail in the Grand Canyon? The spectacular Paria Canyon hike is also missing. How about the trail into Weaver's Needle in the Superstition Mountains and the West Fork of Oak Creek?

Indeed, these and many more hikes not included in this guide are wonderful hikes. But the main purpose of *The Hiker's Guide to Arizona* is to provide an overall review of hiking in Arizona and to introduce hikers to lesser-known areas of the state—the entire state, not just its most-publicized hikes. Nevertheless, we have included those deservedly famous hikes like Aravaipa Canyon which, although quite popular, also feature well-regulated access.

Use this guide book as a starting point to discover your own favorite hikes in the remote corners of the Grand Canyon, Superstition Mountains, Mogollon Rim country, and other wilderness gems of Arizona.

Geology and geography

Imagine yourself in an airplane, swooping down across Arizona from the north—low enough to see mountains, canyons, and forests, yet high enough to see clear across the state, several hundred miles in any direction.

Crossing into Arizona at about the center of the common boundary with Utah, you pass over the southern and western portions of the Colorado Plateau. Though truly a plateau (as opposed to a mountainous region), the Colorado Plateau is anything but flat and featureless. A number of volcanic mountains and uplifts dot the surface, while hundreds of canyons slash deep into sedimentary rocks, draining into a series of master canyons cut by the Colorado River. The river and its canyons so dominate the landscape that the entire Plateau, covering parts of four states, was named after it.

Below you are the lower reaches of Glen Canyon and Lake Powell. To your left, or east, is a fantastic labyrinth of red sandstone canyons, knobs, and fins sprawled around the base of forested, dome-shaped Navajo Mountain. Off to the southeast are the countless red sandstone plateaus and occasional higher forested mesas of the immense Navajo and Hopi Indian reservations, stretching to the base of the Carrizo Mountains along the New Mexico border.

Directly below your speeding plane, the spectacular gorge of Marble Canyon opens to view, sliced through the layer-cake geology of the Colorado Plateau by the Colorado River, which is clearly visible at the bottom of the canyon. Marble Canyon widens before you, a fitting prelude to the greatest of all Colorado River canyons, the Grand Canyon. The high, forested Kaibab Plateau lies to the west, and beyond it, the remote Arizona Strip country, that part of Arizona separated from the rest of the state by the Grand Canyon. Here ancient volcanic cones spewed lava which flowed into Grand Canyon and formed dams and lakes dwarfing any man-made reservoir.

Now the expanse of the Grand Canyon unfolds, wandering more than two hundred river-miles to the west and only ending near the southern tip of Nevada. A classic exposition of geologic strata, the canyon clearly shows how ancient mountains have grown—raised by subterranean pressures which move continents like rafts in the world ocean—only to be destroyed by the seemingly modest forces of wind and water. Rock layers show how great oceans and deserts formed in alternation, not once but several times, each depositing their own unique rocks in distinct horizontal beds.

Southward, you pass over fields of lava flows and a landscape marked with numerous cinder cones and volcanic mountains, finally culminating in the alpine San Francisco Peaks, the highest in the state. Off to the southeast, the Colorado Plateau gradually rises and becomes forested with a rich stand of pines. Abruptly the land drops as you pass over the edge of the Mogollon Rim, which recedes east into the distance. The White Mountains, 9,000-11,000 feet high but gentle and rolling, are visible where the Rim fades into New Mexico.

The edge of the Rim marks the end of the gentler plateau landscape and a transition into the rugged mountain country of central Arizona. A number of deep canyons slash through the Rim, draining into the valleys below. Adjacent mountain ranges, though not high by alpine standards, offer such complex terrain that they are virtual wonderlands of stone, forest, and stream. There are many fine opportunities for backpacking and hiking in this region.

As your airplane continues southward, mountain ranges become lower and farther apart. The city of Phoenix sprawls across a huge desert valley, and the transition to more open terrain is obvious.

To the southwest, the ranges are more desert-like as the general elevation of the land drops. Rugged desert ranges such as the Eagletails and Kofas thrust jagged summits into the sky. To the southeast, the land is generally higher and so are the mountains, reaching 9,000-10,000 feet. Outstanding ranges are the Pinalenos, Chiricahuas, and Galiuros.

This Basin-and-Range topography of alternate mountain ranges and valleys covers the southwestern half of Arizona and large areas of California, Nevada, and Utah. The mountain ranges, some small, some extending a hundred miles or more, trend in a general north-south direction, parallel ranges probably formed by the collision of drifting continental plates which stressed the bedrock. As these stresses increased from the west, the crust of the earth cracked and heaved great blocks of rock upward, often tilting them and dropping the valley floors at the same time. The mountains vary from low, rounded desert hills to alpine peaks with dense forests and permanent streams.

Natural history

Arizona is remarkably rich and diverse in plant and animal life. Habitats range from searing desert to alpine tundra. Annual precipitation can vary from almost none to more than 50 inches. In general the driest areas of the state

2

are the low western and southwestern sections and the wettest regions are the high plateaus and mountains. Arizona typically has two rainy seasons: winter and late summer. At higher elevations (above 5,000 feet) the winter precipitation generally falls as snow. Flagstaff (at 7,000 feet), for example, averages about 80 inches of snow a season. Summer precipitation usually takes the form of afternoon thundershowers which, although generally brief, often result in heavy run-off and flash floods because of the rocky nature of the ground.

The sun shines 85-90 percent of the daytime in Arizona's lower desert regions and only slightly less in higher country. Annual temperature extremes have spanned more than 160 Fahrenheit degrees, from a low of -37 at Maverick to a high of 127 at Parker. Daily fluctuations commonly exceed 40 degrees or more, which is characteristic of arid regions. The normally low humidity allows daytime heat to quickly dissipate at night.

Arizona's plants and animals have evolved communities admirably adapted to surviving under these various, often extreme, environmental conditions. Biologists generally define these communities in terms of the dominant type of vegetation.

Arizona contains six major biotic communities. These, in order of descending altitude, are (1) Alpine Tundra (12,670-11,000 feet); (2) Coniferous Forest, including aspen groves (11,000-6,000 feet); (3) Woodlands (7,000-4,000 feet); (4) Chaparral (6,000-4,000 feet); (5) Grasslands (7,000-4,000 feet); and (6) Deserts (6,000-100 feet). The only major North American biotic community not represented in the state is tropical. In fact, a hike from the summit of the San Francisco Peaks to the bottom of the Grand Canyon, a distance of only eighty miles, is similar in terms of biotic communities to a hike from northern Canada to northern Mexico.

In these six communities are found some 3,370 species of flowering plants, ferns, and fern allies, 64 species of fishes, 22 species of amphibians, 97 species of reptiles, 434 species of birds, and 138 species of mammals. Arizona has 60 percent of all types of wildlife species found in North America. This of course doesn't include the multitude of insects, arachnids, mosses, lichens, and other living organisms that constitute the rest of the ecosystem. Arizona— considered by many people a vast, lifeless desert—actually has a startling abundance of living, breathing, reproducing plants and creatures.

The protection of this wildlife, plantlife, and natural habitat is perhaps the most urgent reason to set aside wilderness areas in Arizona. In addition to the sheer enjoyment and rejuvenation which many people find in observing nature, useful products such as medicines have been developed from native species. Scientists have only begun to discover the wonders of Arizona's indigenous species.

Arizona people

Arizona's earliest human inhabitants were hunters who arrived at least 11,000 years ago, soon after the retreat of the continental glaciers. Those sheets of ice didn't reach as far south as Arizona, but they did affect the climate of the state, producing cooler and wetter weather. Local glaciers, moreover, did exist at higher elevations—in the San Francisco Peaks near Flagstaff, for example.

Arizona's early hunters stalked mammoths, ground sloths, giant bison, Harrington's mountain goats, tapirs (pig-like animals), camels, and other relics of the Pleistocene Age. But after generations of these hunters and a gradual warming and drying of the climate, such species became extinct. The hunters turned their attention to smaller game such as deer, elk, bighorn, antelope, rabbits, squirrels and other rodents, birds, amphibians, reptiles, fishes, and invertebrates. They also placed a greater emphasis on gathering native plants for food. They had to be opportunists to survive in this harsh land.

Approximately four thousand years ago, maize and squash were introduced to Arizona through trade with other peoples to the south, in Mexico. The hunter-gatherers of Arizona gradually became farmers. And as farmers, they tended to stay longer in one place. They didn't have to follow wild herds. Instead they sought out arable land, sowed their seeds, raised their crops, and—in good years—enjoyed bountiful harvests in the fall.

With a more dependable food supply, Arizona's human population slowly began to increase. More people, in turn, engaged in more agriculture. Farming intensified. Three major and distinct Indian cultures developed. People in the southern part of the state, the Hohokam, engineered complex irrigation canals to bring water from the wetter, higher mountains to the desert lowlands. People on the northern plateau, the Anasazi, also farmed but relied mainly on natural precipitation, although they did discover ingenious ways to channel run-off so that the water reached their fields. The Mogollon people, who lived along the central mountain belt, practiced both irrigation and dry farming.

An important addition to the diet of these early Indians occurred about 600-700 A.D., when the bean—a variety very similar to today's pinto bean—was first cultivated. Corn and beans eaten together gave Arizona's early inhabitants a complete source of protein, undoubtedly improving their health and increasing their survival rate. Population boomed.

Life in those days was good. Fields of corn, squash, beans, and cotton grew where cactus or juniper had been. Large villages were constructed of mud, stone, and logs. Indians, living to the ripe old age of thirty or even thirty-five, produced beautiful pottery and developed elaborate religious ceremonies to insure the coming of rain and good fortune.

Then, after six or seven centuries of prosperity, people in the north began having difficulties and started abandoning their homes. What caused their displacement is still not fully understood, but probably involved a combination of extensive drought, overuse of natural resources, overpopulation, and perhaps disease and warfare. By the mid-1400s, people along the Mogollon Rim and southern deserts had also left their villages.

Some of these early peoples moved out of the Arizona region entirely, while others resumed hunting and gathering. A few, such as the Hopi, found locations favorable to their dry-farming methods and continued their agricultural tradition. Also about this same time, new peoples moved into the area, including the Navajo and Apache, primarily nomadic hunting and gathering groups.

In the early 1500s, the first non-Indians arrived upon the scene—Spanish conquistadors looking for gold and other treasures. The first non-Indian to step on Arizona soil was Estevan, a black Moor, who was guiding Fray Marcos de Niza to find legendary golden cities. Soon behind them came the Spanish Fathers looking for heathen souls to save.

Some native American groups fared better than others at repelling the

Spanish invasion. But between 1821 and 1854, Arizona fell under Mexican rule, and by the mid-1850s more intruders were coming—this time American fur trappers, such as James Ohio Pattie, Jedediah Smith, Bill Williams, Pauline Weaver, and Kit Carson. They were followed a few years later by prospectors, ranchers, and settlers.

Conflict erupted as these different people fought over Arizona's limited resources. By the end of the nineteenth century, the Old West was quickly becoming a memory as more territory was settled and new conflicts of interest arose. On Valentine's Day, 1912, Arizona became a state.

Today, Arizona is one of the fastest-growing states. Many retired people seeking refuge from the northern states' severe winters are flocking to the sunny Southwest. The central and southern areas of the state are quickly becoming urbanized and industrialized. Outdoor recreation continues to grow. Only wise planning today will insure that Arizonans will have recreational lands tomorrow.□

HIKING TECHNIQUES AND ETHICS

Touching the land lightly

The American wilderness belongs to all Americans. All of us have the right to enjoy the wilderness, but with that right comes responsibility to take care of the backcountry. Vehicle campers and users of organized recreation areas have come to expect that land managers and forest rangers will maintain recreation sites and clean up after them, but no such services are possible in wilderness areas. Each wilderness user must first of all clean up after himself or herself, and secondly clean up after others who have been careless.

Most wilderness messes appear to be made by people who do not realize how precious and limited wilderness is. Thinking it will be years before anyone passes by again, they leave orange peels strewn about their rest stops,

If you build a campfire, be sure to return the site to its natural condition before leaving. The easiest way is to initially dig a small fire pit into mineral soil. When you are breaking camp, mix the ashes with dirt and water. Make sure the fire is dead out, then cover it with soil and scatter any fire-blackened rocks. Better still, cook on a backpacker's stove and use a candle with foil windbreak as a cheery campfire substitute. Bruce Grubbs

build new campfire rings in campsites already dotted with campfire rings, and try to burn aluminum food packages or bury garbage. Meanwhile another group of hikers is a few days or hours behind, hungry eyes watch from the brush, and aluminum sparkles on the ground as it will for hundreds of years. The golden rule of wilderness—"Leave it the same way you would like to find it"—has been violated again.

Never litter the trail or countryside. Most litter along trails in Arizona is probably accidental, except near heavily populated areas, and many hikers pick up litter when they find it, especially on day hikes or toward the end

Some fires are caused by lightning, including this conflagration near the Kachina Peaks Wilderness Area. Unfortunately, however, many other fires are the result of human carelessness. Since fire restrictions may be imposed on national forests after long dry spells, check with the local ranger before building fires. Stewart Aitchison

of multi-day trips. When setting up camp, note the appearance of the site and resolve to leave it looking as good or better. In particular, avoid excavating tent ditches or large-scale earth-moving to create sleeping sites. Look for areas of sand or pine needles which are naturally smooth and comfortable, instead of digging away at imbedded rocks. With a good sleeping pad, even slabs of rock make excellent campsites.

Campfires account for much of the scarring of campsites. In many heavily used areas, campfires have been permanently prohibited, and in others are prohibited in summer and fall due to the danger of wildfire. Follow such restrictions to the letter. In areas where fires are allowed, you still should not build one if the site is short on firewood or if the wind is blowing. When you do build a fire, avoid building elaborate fire rings and scarring rocks and boulders. Find a site from which it is unlikely the fire can spread, in soft sand or soil. Dig a shallow hole, heaping dirt around the edges. Keep your fire small; and when you leave, fill in the hole with the loose dirt. Do a careful job, and a patch of disturbed soil or sand will be the only evidence you leave behind.

Increasing contamination of wilderness water supplies is a consequence of heavy backcountry use, yet most problems can be prevented with a little common sense. Always answer the call of nature at least 100 yards from any open water, and farther if possible. Dig a hole 4-8 inches deep and bury everything carefully when you are finished. Some people carry a plastic garden trowel to make digging easier.

Preserving our archaeological and historical heritage

Arizona is fortunate to have some of the best-preserved prehistoric structures and artifacts in the world. Unfortunately about 90 percent of the known sites have been vandalized to some degree. Disturbing archaeological sites and

Indian pictographs and petroglyphs are common in Arizona's desert regions. Please help preserve them by not touching them, since the oils in your skin may affect the pigments. Also, sometimes the rock is so friable that a piece may crumble at the slightest touch, and with it a part of history. Stewart Aitchison

artifacts does not simply lessen their scientific value—such activity is essentially grave-robbing.

Two federal laws, the Antiquities Act and the Archaeological Resources Protection Act, forbid removal or destruction of archaeological artifacts and ruins on federal land. An Arizona State Antiquities Act provides similar protection on state lands. Failure to comply with these laws can result in stiff fines and imprisonment. Any vandalism should be immediately reported to the nearest federal or state resource office.

About the maps

Each hike in *The Hiker's Guide to Arizona* is accompanied by a sketch map showing the access road and specific trails mentioned in the hike description. This map should be used only as a general guide, indicating the length and type of hike under discussion. More detailed maps are useful for many hikes described in this book.

One type of more detailed map is the topographic map, or quad, published by the U.S. Geological Survey. These maps come in two basic series, the 7.5-minute and 15-minute quads. The 15-minute quads are generally older maps, sometimes outdated. All newer mapping is being done in the more detailed 7.5-minute series, and these maps show recent roads, trails, and other man-made features. Both series are quite accurate in depicting terrain, which normally does not change significantly. For some areas both 7.5- and 15-minute maps may be available, but generally only one or the other series applies to a specific hike.

A second type of detailed map useful for hikes described here is the National

Learning to use maps is not only fun but essential when exploring much of Arizona's backcountry. Trails are often faint and hard to follow, easy to confuse with livestock and game trails. Some of the state's best wild places can only be reached by cross-country travel with map and compass. Practice map reading by obtaining a U.S. Geological Survey topographic map of an area you are already familiar with, such as your hometown. Bruce Grubbs

Forest and Wilderness map, published by the U.S. Forest Service. Forest Service maps do not show topography, but are updated more often than topographic maps. In addition, roads are more clearly classified as maintained, primitive, or four-wheel-drive roads. Forest road and trail numbers are also shown on these maps, and on Forest Service signs, making it easier to find the trailhead.

Some wilderness maps have been published by the Forest Service. These are based on topographic maps, and the Forest Service has added more up-to-date road and trail information. Where these maps exist, they are very useful. However, they normally don't show the detail that a USGS quad does.

A third type of detailed map mentioned in some descriptions of southern Arizona hikes is published by the Southern Arizona Hiking Club and is available in bookstores and hiking shops in Tucson. These maps are USGS quads with trails marked on them. There are four currently available: Catalinas, Rincons, Santa Ritas, and Chiricahuas.

Learning to read maps is not only fun but, in many cases, also essential in keeping yourself from getting lost. The trail descriptions in *The Hiker's Guide to Arizona* are brief and cannot substitute for good map-reading skills. Moreover, maps not only make our suggested hikes easier to follow, but they also allow you to plan your own original adventures.□

MAKING IT A SAFE TRIP

Backcountry safety

Backpacking and hiking by nature are casual and relaxed sports. However, it is important to remember that the wilderness is totally indifferent to the presence of human visitors. While there are no forces seeking to harm hikers,

Arizona trails such as this one in Whitmore Canyon in western Grand Canyon can be long, steep, dry, and isolated. Never hike alone. Stewart Aitchison

there are none seeking to help them, either. In any kind of wilderness emergency—whether snakebite, a sudden snowstorm, or scorching heat— you are entirely on your own. Even if companions can go for help in an emergency, hours or days may pass before rescuers arrive.

Backcountry safety is largely a matter of common sense. Avoid pushing yourself or members of your party beyond their abilities. Most twisted ankles and broken bones occur because someone was rushing to reach a goal or pushing a slow hiker. Any group can travel safely only as fast as its slowest member.

Plan your trip carefully, allowing extra time to reach each day's campsite (or to return to the car on a day hike). You may be distracted by a side hike or want to spend extra time on a mountain top. If something goes wrong, such as a bad blister, you will have time to take care of the problem. Plan for events such as sudden storms, and consider exit routes where you can abort the trip early if needed.

And take a first aid course!

Dying of thirst

The availability of water governs most backpack trips in Arizona. Most people plan their hikes so that there is water at each campsite and lunch stop, and carry at least two quarts of water. Except during the winter, two quarts is usually a safe minimum, but in hotter weather or when water sources are uncertain, the safe minimum may be four to eight quarts per person per day.

Although topographic and forest maps show springs and running streams, do not count on the water actually being there unless you have a reliable source of information or personal experience which indicates so. Many springs and streams dry up after long dry periods of weather. Be aware of recent weather

A few of Arizona's desert canyons are blessed with permanent streams but most are not. Carry plenty of water and purify any water that you drink from natural sources. Bruce Grubbs

and precipitation, and carry enough water to see you through to the next water source if one happens to be dry.

Keep in mind that it is unnecessary to camp at a water source. Many dry camps are more pleasant than overused, trampled campsites near springs. Besides, your presence may prevent wildlife from coming for a drink—which could be particularly critical during the dry summer months.

There are a number of reliable collapsible water containers on the market. With one of these a hiker can carry enough water from the last spring of the day to last through the night and into the next day, until reaching another water source. And hikers who are not restricted to campsites with water can choose from a spectacular variety of fine campsites—mountaintops, open ridges, and forested glades.

Can I drink it?

No, you can't. It's sad but true that most wilderness water sources are no longer safe to drink. The exceptions are isolated springs and water flowing directly from a fresh snowfield. Increased human use has contaminated most other water sources, and many have been polluted by domestic cattle or wildlife.

Giardiasis, an often-severe gastrointestinal infection caused by a protozoic parasite, has received much attention in the past few years. Land management agencies and backpackers alike have voiced a great deal of concern over the problem. It now seems clear that the protozoa causing Giardiasis is naturally present in many water supplies, including those of many cities, and is spread to wilderness areas by mammals, including man. Not all people are

The floor of Tsegi Canyon on the Navajo Indian Reservation features easy walking, thanks to horizontal beds of sedimentary rocks which occasionally make natural walkways. Stewart Aitchison

affected, but for those who are, the symptoms can be incapacitating.

Iodine tablets such as Globaline or Potable Agua will kill most organisms in water, including *Giardia lamblia* and its cysts. Use one tablet per quart (two if the water is contaminated with decaying organic matter such as leaves), and allow the water to stand for ten minutes (twenty minutes if the water is very cold). According to the third edition of *Medicine for Mountaineering*, even resistant *Giardia* cysts are killed by the concentration of iodine released by these tablets. The iodine tablets must be kept sealed in their original container, however, since any moisture will release the iodine and destroy their effectiveness.

Water filters can also be used for purification, but practical filters require a pump for a reasonable output of water and, until recently, seemed too heavy and expensive for backpacking. Newer, lighter designs are becoming available, however. Chlorine tablets are less effective on wilderness water sources because of organic matter in the water which is removed in city water systems.

Freezing to death

It may seem strange to talk about hypothermia in a state as hot as Arizona, but much outdoor recreation in the state takes place in higher areas or during cooler times of the year. Especially in winter and early spring, sudden storms can drop snow on deserts as low as 2,000 feet and several feet of snow can accumulate at higher elevations. Snow is possible between October and May above 5,000 feet and anytime of the year above 9,000 feet, and a number of hikers who were unprepared for such conditions have died.

Before leaving on your trip, get the immediate and long-range weather

When entering narrow canyons, be aware of the potential for rain and sudden run-off to create a raging flash flood. Remember that a storm which is far out of sight upstream while you hike under cloudless skies may nevertheless pose a life-threatening hazard. Never camp in the bottom of a dry wash. Bruce Grubbs

forecasts. Delay or reschedule your trip if a major winter storm is forecast. Plan alternate routes and escape routes on longer trips. Learn to read weather from the wind and the sky. An experienced hiker can predict the weather surprisingly well from just these natural signs, and rarely does an approaching storm arrive without some warning signs.

Learn, too, the symptoms of hypothermia and how to prevent it. With modern clothing and by layering that clothing, it is possible to hike in inclement weather with a considerable margin of safety.□

THE HIKES

These sixty hikes offer a variety of landscapes, difficulty, and length. Most can be day trips for anyone in good physical condition, many can be made into longer backpacks, and several are epic adventures for the hardy and prepared.

A word about difficulty: Our ratings system for the degree of difficulty of these hikes is, of course, subjective. The difficulty of a particular hike can be influenced by much more than the trail itself—weather, for instance, or the physical condition of the hiker. Yet even generalizations about difficulty can be valuable for hikers unfamiliar with a particular trail, and so *The Hiker's Guide to Arizona* ranks hikes as easy, moderate, or difficult. An easy hike has little elevation gain or loss, is relatively short, and requires a minimum of map-reading skill. A moderate hike has significant elevation gain or loss, is longer or requires more time, may include sections of cross-country travel, and basic map-reading skills are helpful. A difficult hike either (1) has elevation gains or losses of several thousand feet or more, (2) entails hiking eight miles or more per day, and/or (3) requires advanced topographic map-reading skills.

There are, of course, many other hiking possibilities in addition to those included in *The Hiker's Guide to Arizona,* and part of the fun of hiking is discovering your own favorite places. After gaining some experience on these trails, study topographic and Forest Service maps, join a local hiking club, and plan your own adventures. Arizona's wild places are waiting. Happy Trails!

The Arizona Trail

A topographic map of Arizona reveals a corridor of high country that trends north and south from the Utah border to Mexico. A project is underway to develop an "Arizona Trail" that will allow foot and horse travelers to traverse the length of the state through this natural corridor.

The initial phase in the creation of the Arizona Trail will be the linking of existing trails and unpaved roads. Priorities for new trail construction will then be formulated so that, eventually, the route will be entirely on-trail.

It is difficult to determine the exact route the Arizona Trail will take. A survey of the state suggests many attractions that should be part of the trail. The final choice will consist of a main trail through diverse landscapes and spur trails leading to scenic sidetrips.

Though the detail work is still underway, the following areas are likely to be integrated into the Arizona Trail. From south to north, they include

Scattered around the base of the Beaver Dam Mountains are stands of Joshua trees, members of the lily family. The striking bloom is pollinated only by the yucca moth, which in turn depends upon the plant to provide a nesting place and food for the moth's caterpillars—a perfect example of a symbiotic relationship. Stewart Aitchison

the Coronado Memorial and Huachuca Mountains, Rincon and Santa Catalina Mountains, Superstition Mountains, Mazatzal Mountains, the Mogollon Rim, Anderson Mesa, San Francisco Mountains, the old stage coach route to the Grand Canyon, South and North Kaibab Trails, and the Kaibab Plateau.

For hikers who thrive on the variety of life zones unique to Arizona, the Arizona Trail will provide a delightful challenge.— *Dale Shewalter*

(For updates on Arizona Trail development, contact Dale Shewalter, P.O. Box 562, Flagstaff, AZ 86002. During the summer of 1985, Shewalter walked the length of Arizona in twenty-one days and has become the main force behind the creation of the Arizona Trail.)

HIKE 1 *BEAVER DAM MOUNTAINS*

General description: Short round-trip day hike into the Beaver Dam Mountains Wilderness Area.
General location: Eight miles northeast of Littlefield.
Maps: Littlefield 15-minute USGS quad; BLM Paiute Primitive Area map.
Difficulty: Easy (cross-country).
Length: As much as three miles one way.
Elevations: 2,700 to 2,900 feet.
Special attractions: Joshua trees, desert tortoises, solitude.
Water availability: None.
Best season: Spring and fall.
For more information: Bureau of Land Management, Arizona Strip District Office, 196 East Tabernacle, St. George, UT 84770; (801) 673-3545.
Permit: None.

This hike begins at the Cedar Pocket Rest Stop on Interstate 15 about 8 miles northeast of Littlefield. There are no established trails in the Beaver Dam Mountains, but it is an easy stroll through the beautiful Joshua tree forest to the base of the mountains. A short walk here is a great introduction to the unique and occasionally bizarre flora and fauna of the Mojave and Great Basin deserts. Adventurous hikers can gain access to the Beaver Dam range itself by traveling cross-country up any of the boulder-strewn drainages.

Joshua trees are related to yuccas and therefore are members of the lily family. These trees are typical of the Mojave Desert, but here Mojave Desert species are intermingled with Great Basin species.

Joshua trees do not bloom every year—the interval between blooms is determined by rainfall and temperature. The species' name was given by Mormons who thought the trees seemed to be lifting their "arms" in supplication as did the Biblical Joshua. Paiutes wove the small red roots of Joshua trees into baskets to make designs.

If you are lucky, you may see the endangered desert tortoise. You will certainly encounter Gambel's quail. The name of these mountains comes from the beaver lodges that were to be found along the main drainage on the western side of the range, near present-day Littlefield.—*Stewart Aitchison* □

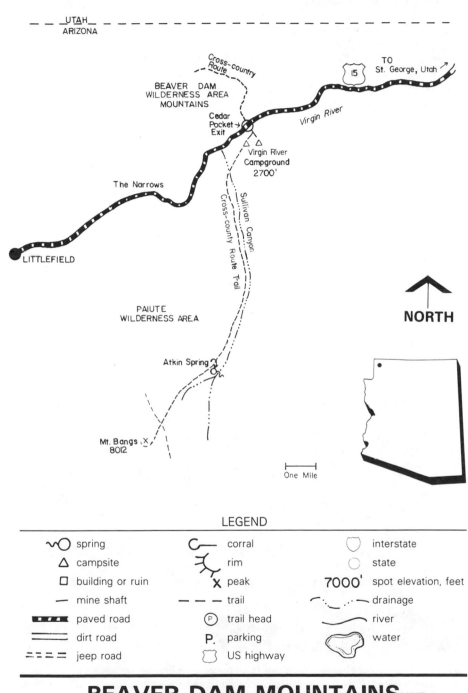

UTAH
ARIZONA

Cross-country Route

BEAVER DAM
WILDERNESS AREA
MOUNTAINS

Cedar
Pocket
Exit

15 TO
St. George, Utah

Virgin River

△ △

Virgin River
Campground
2700'

The Narrows

Sullivan Canyon

Cross-county Route Trail

LITTLEFIELD

PAIUTE
WILDERNESS AREA

Atkin Spring

Mt. Bangs X
8012

One Mile

NORTH

LEGEND

∿○	spring	C—	corral	⬡	interstate
△	campsite	⫚	rim	◯	state
▢	building or ruin	X	peak	**7000'**	spot elevation, feet
—	mine shaft	– – –	trail	⌁	drainage
▰▰▰	paved road	Ⓟ	trail head	～	river
══	dirt road	P.	parking	▱	water
≡≡≡	jeep road	⬠	US highway		

BEAVER DAM MOUNTAINS HIKE 1
MOUNT BANGS HIKE 2

HIKE 2 *MOUNT BANGS*

General description: Long round-trip overnighter to the highest point in the Paiute Wilderness Area.
General location: Eight miles southeast of Littlefield.
Maps: Littlefield 15-minute USGS quad.
Difficulty: Difficult (mostly cross-country).
Length: About 12 miles one way.
Elevation: 2,700 to 8,012 feet.
Special attractions: Fantastic views of three states from the summit.
Water availability: None until Atkin Spring.
Best season: Spring and fall.
For more information: Bureau of Land Management, Arizona Strip District Office, 196 East Tabernacle, St. George, UT 84770; (801) 673-3545.
Permit: None.

To find the trailhead, drive about 20 miles southwest of St. George, Utah on Interstate 15. Exit at the Virgin River Campground. On the south side of the campground, ford the Virgin River. Then walk about 1.5 miles downstream to the mouth of Sullivan Canyon. The route up the canyon is rough and rocky now, although a trail is planned for the future. Near the head of Sullivan Canyon, climb west up through the natural break, West Fork Gate, to Atkin Spring. A trail from the spring leads southwesterly toward Mount Bangs. About a mile before reaching the summit, the trail divides. One branch goes north as the Virgin Ridge Trail; a second goes south to what is called the South Trailhead in Cottonwood Wash; and a third trail, which you follow, goes

The handsome collared lizard is frequently seen basking on boulders in Arizona's wildlands. Male lizards found in the Colorado Plateau area of northern Arizona are usually a striking blue-green color, while those found in the low deserts of southern and western Arizona are often brown. Males, such as this one, are usually brighter than females. When alarmed, the collared lizard may flee by running on only its hind legs. Stewart Aitchison

toward Mount Bangs. In another mile, the trail ends on the ridge that runs up to the summit of Mount Bangs, the goal and turnaround point of this hike.

Along the way you may encounter bighorn sheep. They were indigenous here at one time, but had disappeared from the range by the 1930s. In 1981 bighorns from the Kingman area were transplanted to this mountain range.

The Virgin Mountains stand between two great geologic provinces, the Basin and Range region to the west and the Colorado Plateau to the east. The route begins in a mix of Great Basin and Mohave desert plants such as Joshua trees and sagebrush, then moves up through pinyon-juniper woodland to an island of ponderosa pine. Mount Bangs, which was named by the eminent geologist Clarence Dutton after his clerk James E. Bangs, supports a small stand of Douglas fir and white fir.—*Stewart Aitchison* ☐

HIKE 3   *MOUNT LOGAN*

General description: Short, round-trip day hike in the Mount Logan Wilderness Area.

General location: Eighty miles south of St. George, Utah and 55 miles southwest of Fredonia.

Maps: Mt. Logan 7.5-minute, Mt. Trumbull NW 7.5-minute USGS quads; Kaibab National Forest map.

Difficulty: Easy (cross-country).

Length: About 1.5 miles one way.

Elevation: 7,300 to 7,866 feet.

Special attractions: Merriam's turkeys.

Water availability: None.

Best season: Spring through fall.

For more information: Bureau of Land Management, Arizona Strip District Office, 196 East Tabernacle, St. George, UT 84770; (801) 673-3545.

Permit: None.

Mount Logan can be reached via the Toroweap Road that exits Arizona 389, 8 miles west of Fredonia. After about 46 miles of dirt road, you will come to a major fork in the road. Take the right branch heading west toward Mount Trumbull. Just before the Nixon Spring reservoir and corral, turn left (south) and drive about 4 miles to a major fork. The right fork used to continue to the top of Mount Logan but should now be closed to vehicles since the area beyond is a wilderness area.

Hike along the old road about a mile, then cut off cross-country uphill to reach the summit and a spectacular view into the eroded west side of the mountain called Hells Hole. In 1858, Lt. Joseph Christmas Ives called this volcanic range the North Side Mountains, a reference to the fact that these mountains are on the north side of the Grand Canyon. Fourteen years later, Maj. John Wesley Powell christened this peak after U.S. Senator John Logan.

Like Mounts Trumbull and Emma, Mount Logan is an extinct volcano. This section of the Arizona Strip Country was the scene of tremendous volcanic activity during the late Cenozoic time. Lava flows filled entire canyons and even spilled into the Grand Canyon, damming the Colorado River.—*Stewart Aitchison* ☐

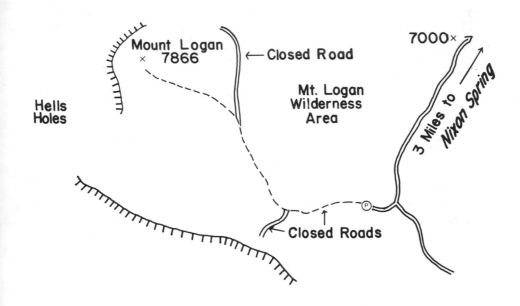

Mount Logan
7866 ×

← Closed Road

Hells
Holes

Mt. Logan
Wilderness
Area

7000 ×

3 Miles to *Nixon Spring*

← Closed Roads

Ⓟ

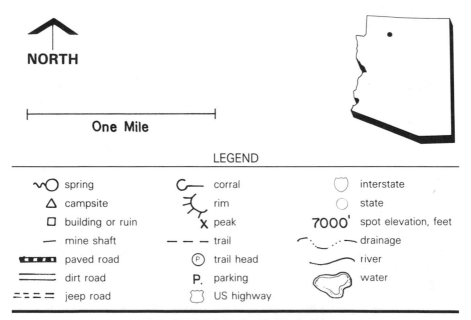

NORTH

One Mile

LEGEND

∿○	spring	C—	corral	◯	interstate	
△	campsite	⊻	rim	◯	state	
☐	building or ruin	X	peak	7000'	spot elevation, feet	
—	mine shaft	– – –	trail	⌣	drainage	
▩	paved road	Ⓟ	trail head	⌢	river	
=	dirt road	P.	parking	◯	water	
= = =	jeep road	⌂	US highway			

MOUNT LOGAN HIKE 3

HIKE 4 *MOUNT TRUMBULL*

General description: A short round-trip day hike on an ancient volcano in the Mount Trumbull Wilderness Area.

General Location: Eighty miles south of St. George, Utah, and 55 miles southwest of Fredonia.

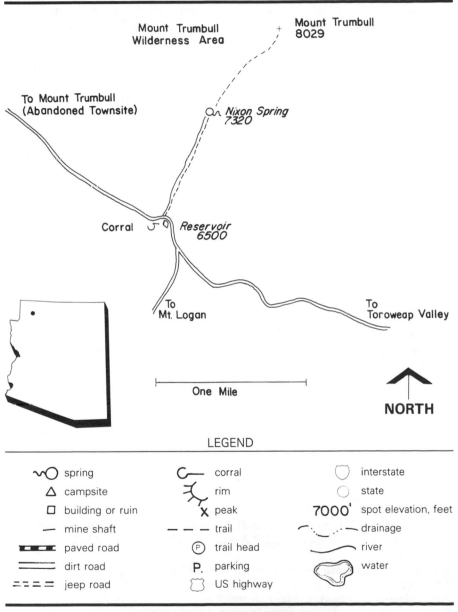

Mount Trumbull
Wilderness Area

Mount Trumbull
8029

To Mount Trumbull
(Abandoned Townsite)

Nixon Spring
7320

Corral

Reservoir
6500

To
Mt. Logan

To
Toroweap Valley

One Mile

NORTH

LEGEND

spring	corral	interstate	
campsite	rim	state	
building or ruin	peak	7000' spot elevation, feet	
mine shaft	trail	drainage	
paved road	trail head	river	
dirt road	parking	water	
jeep road	US highway		

MOUNT TRUMBULL HIKE 4

Maps: Mount Trumbull NW 7.5-minute USGS quad; Kaibab National Forest map.
Difficulty: Easy.
Length: About 1.5 miles one way.
Elevation: 6,400 to 8,028 feet.
Special attractions: Historic sites and the unique Kaibab squirrel.
Water availability: Nixon Spring usually has water.
Best season: Spring through fall.
For more information: Bureau of Land Management, Arizona Strip District Office, 196 East Tabernacle, St. George, UT 84770; (801) 673-3545.
Permit: None.

Mount Trumbull is accessible via the Toroweap Road that branches off of Arizona 389, 8 miles west of Fredonia. After about 46 miles of dirt road, you will come to a major fork in the road. Take the right branch heading west toward Mount Trumbull.

In about 6 miles you will come to Nixon Springs, the site of a steam-powered sawmill built by Mormons in 1870. An interpretive sign marks the location. Here, Mormons cut ponderosa timbers for the construction of the St. George Temple. The timbers were hauled by oxen over 80 miles to St. George. The wagon ruts are still visible today.

The trail heads up the mountain where a wooden flume used to carry water from a spring down to the mill. To reach the summit of Mount Trumbull, the goal and turnaround point of this hike, you should continue upslope. A good trail takes you to the summit for a grand view of the Arizona Strip Country.

Kaibab squirrels, a strikingly handsome beast endemic to the North Rim of the Grand Canyon, were introduced on Mount Trumbull in the 1970s. These tassel-eared fellows eat ponderosa pine seeds and certain fungi associated with the pines.

Mount Trumbull was named after U.S. Senator Lyman Trumbull by Major John Wesley Powell during his exploration of the Arizona Strip in 1871-1872.

Except during the deer hunting season, the hiker is unlikely to encounter anyone in this area.—*Stewart Aitchison* □

HIKE 5 *SURPRISE CANYON*

General description: A round-trip day hike or backpack into a remote part of the Grand Canyon.
General location: About 50 miles northeast of Kingman.
Maps: Spencer Canyon 7.5-minute, Devils Slide Rapid 7.5- minute, Amos Point 7.5-minute, Mount Dellenbaugh 7.5-minute, Whitmore Point SW 7.5-minute USGS quads.
Difficulty: Moderate to difficult (cross-country).
Length: Fourteen miles or more one way.
Elevation: 1,250 to 3,500 feet or more.
Special attractions: Remoteness, incredible geology.
Water availability: A stream flows intermittently along the canyon floor.

Best season: Fall through spring.
For more information: Grand Canyon National Park, P.O. Box 129, Grand Canyon, AZ 86023; (602) 638-2474.
Permit: Required from National Park Service for overnight camping.
Wilderness status: Administratively endorsed wilderness.

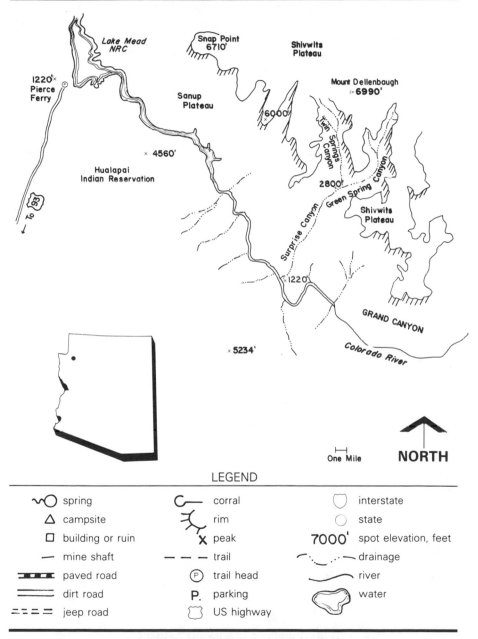

LEGEND

∿○	spring	C—	corral	⬡	interstate
△	campsite	⋇	rim	○	state
☐	building or ruin	X	peak	**7000'**	spot elevation, feet
—	mine shaft	— — —	trail	⌒··⌒	drainage
▬▬▬	paved road	Ⓟ	trail head	⌒⌒	river
═══	dirt road	P.	parking	⬭	water
‗ ‗ ‗	jeep road	⬭	US highway		

SURPRISE CANYON HIKE 5

This trip is unique in that it requires a boat to reach the trailhead. If you have launched your boat from Pierce Ferry on Lake Mead, you will need to cruise about 32 miles upstream to reach the mouth of Surprise Canyon.

One of the canyon's surprises is the sand bar that sometimes forms at the canyon's mouth. This bar can prevent your boat from entering the canyon if the lake level is down.

The canyon may have received its name from the large area that drains into such an inconspicuous slot through the granite at the river. The creek is also exceptional in that it is not necessary to carry water for the long (about 14-mile) trailless hike up to the junction with Twin Springs Canyon. Water runs on the surface and then disappears, but you are never more than forty-five minutes from where the water reappears.

The walking is slow because of flood-scattered boulders. Some wading may be necessary. Take special care of the footing—hikers have suffered nasty falls here.

Surprise Canyon has several fine overhangs that will shelter you on a wet night, especially near the top of the Tapeats Sandstone and in the Redwall Limestone near the junction with Twin Springs Canyon.

Surprise Canyon has so many intriguing features that it has become a favorite haunt of mine. For instance, there is a natural bridge on the east side about .3 mile up the bed from the west border of the Amos Point quad. From a little distance, this place looks like a simple overhang and there is no big drainage in it.

The many sidecanyons invite exploration. Some have fantastic narrows cut into the Redwall Limestone. About a mile up Twin Springs Canyon, you reach the narrowest and deepest Redwall gorge I have ever seen. Others, such as the Green Spring Arm, contain pools that require swimming.

This is a great place for the exploratory hiker.—*Harvey Butchart* □

Editors' note: Harvey Butchart is *the* authority on hiking in the Grand Canyon area. This trail description has been paraphrased from his extensive hiking notes that cover over forty years of Grand Canyon exploration.

HIKE 6 *HACK CANYON*

General description: A round-trip day hike in the Kanab Creek Wilderness Area.

General location: Thirty-five miles south of Fredonia, off the Mount Trumbull-Toroweap Road.

Maps: Heaton Knolls 15-minute, Jumpup Canyon 15-minute USGS quads.

Difficulty: Moderate.

Length: About 2 miles one way.

Elevation: 5,100 to 3,900 feet.

Special attractions: Access to spectacular Kanab Canyon and its sidecanyons.

Water: Willow Spring.

Best season: Spring and fall.

For more information: Bureau of Land Management, Arizona Strip District Office, 196 East Tabernacle, St. George, UT 84770; (801) 673-3545.

Permit: None unless camping within Grand Canyon National Park.

From Fredonia, drive west on Arizona 389 about 8 miles to the Toroweap Road. Drive south about 30 miles on this graded dirt road. Two miles before crossing the low ridge at CCC Trail Reservoir (the Heaton Knolls map will be useful), turn south and follow the best road about 6 miles to the rim of Hack Canyon. The road now turns east and follows the rim. Watch for a small corral out on the very rim of the canyon about a mile east of the point where the road met the rim. The Hack Canyon Trail starts from this corral.

From the corral, the trail descends west a short distance, then switchbacks to the east below the rim cliffs. It works its way through a break in the buff-colored Coconino Sandstone cliff, then drops onto a broad talus fan and descends directly to the bed of Hack Canyon. A few hundred yards upstream is Willow Spring on the south bank. The spring seems to be reliable but should be purified. From the spring, it is an easy walk downstream to Kanab Canyon, the turnaround point for this hike but an excellent starting point for your own exploratory hikes.

The Hack Trail is a good access route for extended trips in the Kanab Canyon-Jumpup Canyon area. You enter Grand Canyon National Park at Jumpup Canyon, and a permit is required for camping within the park. The Hack Trail was probably built by cattle ranchers for access to Willow Spring, which is a valuable source of water on the dry Arizona Strip.

The area is part of a BLM wilderness area established in 1984. A few miles upstream of Willow Spring, an old uranium mine has been reopened with possible impacts on the remote character of the Arizona Strip. For example, the miners would like to see the Toroweap Road paved to improve all-weather access to the mine area.—*Bruce Grubbs* □

Kanab Creek is the major north-side drainage to the Grand Canyon and has numerous side-canyons which provide endless possibilities for exploration. Bruce Grubbs

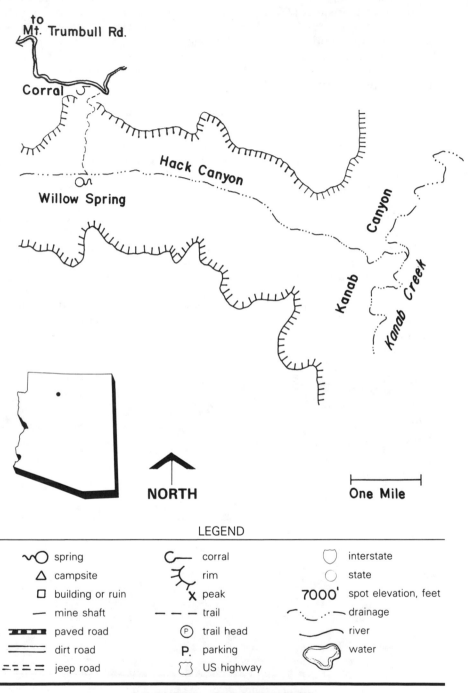

to
Mt. Trumbull Rd.

Corral

Hack Canyon

Willow Spring

Kanab Canyon

Kanab Creek

NORTH

One Mile

LEGEND

⌀○	spring	ℭ—	corral	⬡	interstate
△	campsite		rim	○	state
▢	building or ruin	X	peak	7000'	spot elevation, feet
—	mine shaft	– – –	trail		drainage
▰▰▰	paved road	Ⓟ	trail head		river
═══	dirt road	P.	parking		water
≡≡≡	jeep road		US highway		

HACK CANYON HIKE 6

HIKE 7 JUMPUP CANYON

General description: A round-trip two- or three-day backpack in Kanab Creek Wilderness Area.
General location: Twenty-five miles south of Fredonia.
Maps: Jumpup Canyon 15-minute, Kanab Point 15-minute USGS quads; Kaibab National Forest North map.
Difficulty: Moderate to difficult (cross-country).
Length: About 10 miles one way to Kanab Canyon.
Elevation: 5,600 to 2,600 feet.
Special attractions: Scenic and remote access to Kanab Creek in western Grand Canyon.
Water: Lower Jumpup Spring, near Kanab Creek.
Best season: Spring and fall.
For more information: North Kaibab Ranger District, P.O. Box 248, Fredonia, AZ 86022; (602) 643-5895.
Permit: Required downstream of confluence of Jumpup and Kanab creeks within Grand Canyon National Park.

Jumpup Canyon is one of the many scenic arms of Kanab Creek. Much of this area has been recently added to Grand Canyon National Park. Additional areas in Jumpup and upper Kanab Canyons have been protected as wilderness administered by the Forest Service and Bureau of Land Management.

Turn off U.S. 89A about 25 miles east of Fredonia and go south on Forest Road 422A. About 12 miles south of the highway, turn west (right) on Forest Road 423 and follow this road to its end in Jumpup Canyon. There are many forks, so follow the road signs carefully. This road is normally passable to high-clearance vehicles except in winter or early spring.

An old cabin marks the end of the road, and the Jumpup Trail starts from the east side of the old corral and immediately starts down the canyon. After about a mile the trail reaches the canyon floor, and a sign points out Jumpup Spring. This spring is not reliable.

Although the Forest Service map shows Trail 41 continuing down Jumpup Canyon, it no longer exists for practical purposes. However, it is easy walking down the dry gravel streambed about 4 miles to Lower Jumpup Spring, which is reliable.

Below Lower Jumpup Spring, the stream bed normally has running water, and the walking gets somewhat rougher. In the red Supai Sandstone formation, you come to a high waterfall, bypassing it on the southeast. You will probably need to lower your packs on a rope. About 2 miles below Lower Jumpup Spring, you come to Sowats Canyon on the left (east). In another mile you pass the entrance to Kwagunt Hollow and in yet another mile, the entrance to Indian Hollow. These are all interesting and beautiful canyons to explore.

From Sowats Canyon, it is about 5 miles to Kanab Creek. Much of this section is in spectacular narrows cut through the Redwall Limestone. In comparison, Kanab Canyon seems almost spacious. The narrows is usually dry but is subject to dangerous flash flooding and should not be hiked if water is running or there is any danger of rain in the headwaters. About a mile above the junction with Kanab Canyon, a pothole below a dry waterfall on the right usually has water. Kanab Creek has permanent water a couple of miles below

Jumpup Creek, and is the turnaround point for a two- or three-day round-trip hike.

South of Jumpup Creek you enter Grand Canyon National Park and a permit is required for overnight camping within the Park. Many more days can be spent exploring the side canyons of Jumpup and Kanab canyons. Jumpup is but an introduction to this fine area.— *Bruce Grubbs* □

HIKE 8 *NORTH CANYON*

General description: A round-trip day hike into the Saddle Mountain Wilderness Area.
General location: Twenty miles north of the North Rim of the Grand Canyon.
Maps: DeMotte Park 15-minute USGS quad; Kaibab National Forest map.
Difficulty: Moderate.
Length: Six miles or less one way.
Elevation: 7,540 to 8,800 feet.
Special attractions: Apache trout in the small stream.
Water availability: A small permanent stream.
Best season: Summer and fall.
For more information: North Kaibab Ranger District, P.O. Box 248, Fredonia, AZ 86022; (602) 643-5895.
Permit: None for hiking; valid Arizona license for fishing.

This hike offers amazing views from the Kaibab Plateau into House Rock Valley and the Marble Canyon area. Hikers may also fish for the rare Apache trout, which is endemic to the White Mountains of east-central Arizona but has recently been stocked here.

To find the trailhead, go about 1.5 miles south of the Kaibab Lodge and turn left onto Forest Road 611. Follow 611 about 4 miles to the East Rim Viewpoint.

The trail begins here and switchbacks steeply down into North Canyon, visible below during your descent. If you follow the trail all 6 miles, you pass through a number of different life zones or plant communities—from spruce-fir forest down to sagebrush desert. The maples and other deciduous trees along the creek are exceptionally beautiful during the fall.

The trail ends at Forest Road 631.—*Gary Russell* □

HIKE 9 *JACOB'S POOLS*

General description: A round-trip day hike following remnants of an old trail into the Paria Canyon-Vermilion Cliffs Wilderness Area.
General location: Twenty miles east of Jacob Lake.
Maps: Emmett Wash 15-minute USGS quad.
Difficulty: Moderate (mostly cross-country).
Length: About 3 miles one way.

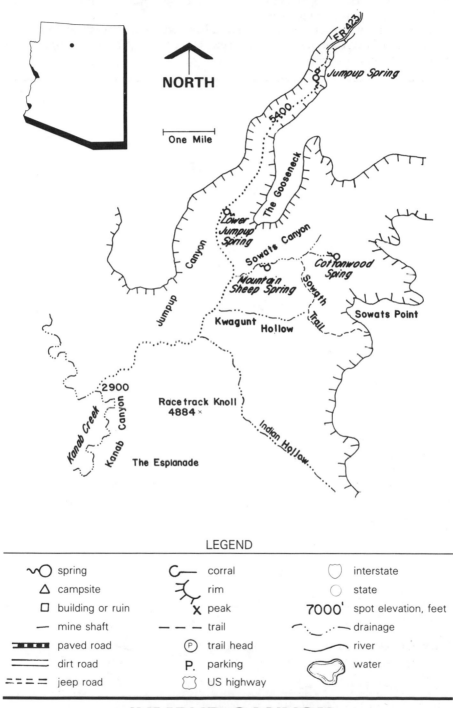

NORTH

One Mile

FR 423

Jumpup Spring

5400

The Gooseneck

Lower Jumpup Spring

Jumpup Canyon

Sowats Canyon

Cottonwood Spring

Mountain Sheep Spring

Sowats Trail

Sowats Point

Kwagunt Hollow

2900

Racetrack Knoll 4884 ×

Kanab Creek

Kanab Canyon

Indian Hollow

The Esplanade

LEGEND

∿〇	spring	C	corral	〇	interstate
△	campsite	〣	rim	〇	state
☐	building or ruin	✗	peak	7000'	spot elevation, feet
—	mine shaft	– – –	trail	⌒⋯⌒	drainage
▰▰▰	paved road	℗	trail head	⌒⌒	river
══	dirt road	P.	parking	⬡	water
≡≡≡	jeep road	�	US highway		

JUMPUP CANYON HIKE 7

Elevation: 5,200 to 6,800 feet.
Special attractions: Spectacular views of House Rock Valley.
Best season: Fall through spring.
For more information: Bureau of Land Management, Arizona Strip District Office, 196 East Tabernacle, St. George, UT 84770; (801) 673-3545.
Permit: None.

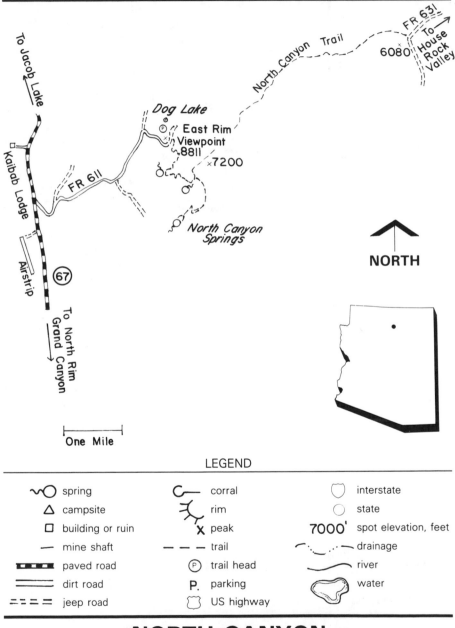

LEGEND

∿◯	spring	ᑖ⎯	corral	◯	interstate
△	campsite	⋎	rim	◯	state
☐	building or ruin	X	peak	7000'	spot elevation, feet
⎯	mine shaft	– – –	trail	⌒⋯⋯⌒	drainage
▰▰▰▰	paved road	℗	trail head	⌒⌒	river
═══	dirt road	P.	parking	◯	water
≡≡≡	jeep road	☁	US highway		

NORTH CANYON HIKE 8

This primitive, unmaintained trail is about 20 miles east of Jacob Lake. Turn off U.S. 89A just west of milepost 557, which is about two hundred yards east of an historical marker. Follow this road past the corral over the hill and down into the area where plastic tubes bring water from the seeps in the clay hills down to the pool.

In places where trails are intermittent or non-existent, human or animal tracks are often the next-best thing. On this hike, for instance, I followed the footprints of three or four people going up the sandy slope toward the break in the rim above. When I was about halfway up the whole slope, I went to the south because I found some cairns in that direction; the tracks I had been observing, however, went more directly up. Before I had gone far enough south to use the man-made trail to the top, I followed deer tracks up through the broken slope consisting of sand and loose rocks. When I was nearing the final narrow ravine through the top cliff, I recognized a well-built retaining wall and realized that I was finally on the right route.

I noticed the "G.M. Wright, 20 April 1894" inscription right away and also quite a few very old pecked-in petroglyphs stained with desert varnish, an iron or manganese oxide deposit. I made it *to the top* in 1 hour, 45 minutes. Before turning around, I also saw other petroglyphs and a wild beehive in a fissure in the cliff right near some of the best rock art.

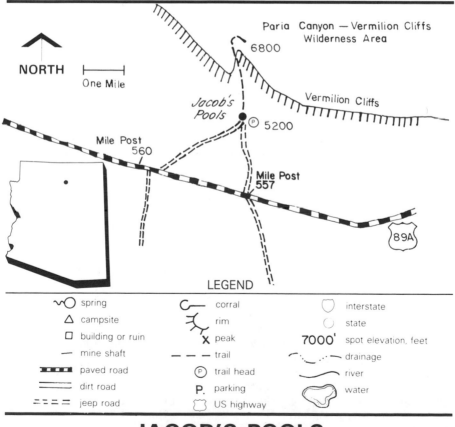

Paria Canyon — Vermilion Cliffs Wilderness Area

NORTH

One Mile

6800

Jacob's Pools

Vermilion Cliffs

5200

Mile Post 560

Mile Post 557

89A

LEGEND

spring	corral	interstate	
campsite	rim	state	
building or ruin	peak	7000' spot elevation, feet	
mine shaft	trail	drainage	
paved road	trail head	river	
dirt road	parking	water	
jeep road	US highway		

JACOB'S POOLS HIKE 9

Descending, I was able to detect and follow more of the old trail. Incidentally, I also saw more recent inscriptions than the one of 1894. Someone had scratched "Spence" on the wall with the date 1941.—*Harvey Butchart*

Editors note: Harvey Butchart is the authority on hiking in the Grand Canyon area. This trail description has been paraphrased from his notes of an exploratory trip to Jacob's Pool.

HIKE 10 *SALIENT POINT*

General description: Very remote round-trip day hike in the Paria Canyon-Vermilion Cliffs Wilderness Area.
General location: West of Marble Canyon.
Maps: Paria Plateau 15-minute, Lees Ferry 15-minute, House Rock Spring 15-minute USGS quads.
Difficulty: Easy.
Length: About a mile one way.
Elevation: 7,000 to 7,200 feet.
Special attractions: Rare and spectacular view of Marble Canyon.
Water: None.
Best season: April through October.
For more information: Bureau of Land Management, Arizona Strip District Office, 196 East Tabernacle, St. George, UT 84770; (801) 673-3545.
Permit: None.

This long drive and short hike takes you to the rim of the Vermilion Cliffs above Marble Canyon and is well worth the trip for the expansive view. Leave U.S. 89A at House Rock (just before the ascent west onto the Kaibab Plateau), and drive north on a good dirt road about 10 miles to another road going east (right) onto the Paria Plateau. This road becomes very sandy a short distance after the junction and four wheel drive is necessary. It will be necessary to use the maps closely to find the remainder of the route.

When the road drops into Pinnacle Valley, go south to a steel stock tank, then east-northeast on the main road to Joes Ranch. About .5 mile west of the ranch, a fork goes south at a stock tank. Stay on this to the end at a stock tank below some white cliffs. The road is shown correctly on the topos except for the turnoff at Joes Ranch.

Walk south onto the mesa and continue cross-country .75 mile to the highest point of the rim, your turnaround point and marked by the "Salient" benchmark. There are places to camp, but you will have to carry water.

The Vermilion Cliffs are formed of Navajo Sandstone, a formation of petrified sand dunes responsible for much of the red rock desert of northern Arizona and southern Utah. The top surface of the sandstone has eroded into deep and loose sand, making the roads in this area difficult or impossible without four-wheel drive. Most of the Paria Plateau north of the Cliffs is covered with pinyon-juniper forest, but ponderosa pines are found in the highest areas. There are many interesting places to explore in the Paria Canyon-Vermilion Cliffs Wilderness Area: famous ones like Paria Canyon and unknown ones like Coyote Buttes.—*Bruce Grubbs* □

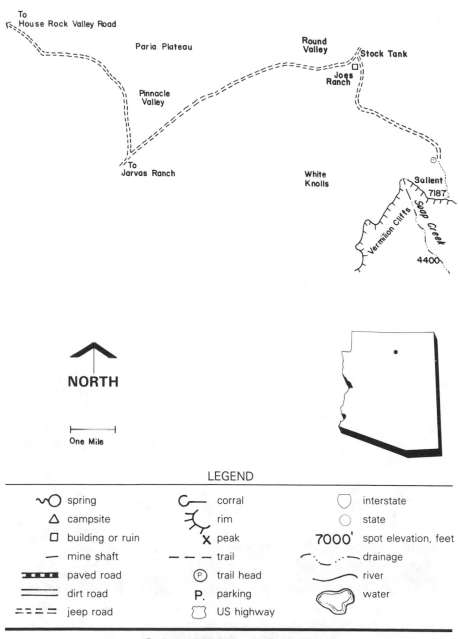

To
House Rock Valley Road

Paria Plateau

Round
Valley

Stock Tank

Joes
Ranch

Pinnacle
Valley

To
Jarvas Ranch

White
Knolls

Salient
7187

Vermilion Cliffs

Soap Creek

4400

NORTH

One Mile

LEGEND

∿○	spring	C⌐	corral	◌	interstate	
△	campsite	⋇	rim	○	state	
◻	building or ruin	X	peak	**7000'**	spot elevation, feet	
—	mine shaft	– – –	trail	⌒‥⌒	drainage	
▪▬▪▬▪	paved road	Ⓟ	trail head	∿	river	
══	dirt road	P.	parking	◇	water	
＝＝＝	jeep road	⬔	US highway			

SALIENT POINT HIKE 10

HIKE 11 *BLUE SPRINGS*

General description: A round-trip day hike or backpack into the remote Little Colorado River Gorge.

General location: Thirty miles northwest of Cameron.

Maps: Vishnu Temple 15-minute, Blue Springs 15-minute USGS quads.

Difficulty: Extremely rugged, borders on climbing.

Length: About 1.5 miles one way.

Elevation: 5,400 to 3,200 feet.

Special attractions: A little-used route into a weird canyon.

Water availability: Blue Springs is permanent but highly mineralized.

Best season: Spring and fall.

For more information: Grand Canyon National Park, P.O. Box 129, Grand Canyon, AZ 86023; (602) 638-2474.

Permit: Technically a permit is required from the Navajo Tribe since this trail is on the reservation; however, since ingress is usually made through Grand Canyon National Park, the park service has issued permits in the past.

Wilderness status: None (Navajo Reservation).

Finding this trailhead is nearly as challenging as the hike. You can approach it either by starting at Desert View within Grand Canyon National Park or heading north off of Arizona 64. In either case, the idea is to eventually end up due east of Gold Butte. (The first time I tried to find this trail, I ended up in one drainage south of the proper one. We got part-way down, but then were cliffed out.) It is really quite hopeless to decribe the driving route since

Most of the Blue Springs route is more scramble than hike. This is not a trip for beginning hikers, nor for those who suffer from vertigo. But for the experienced backpacker, Blue Springs and other sections of the Little Colorado River Gorge offer splendid wilderness adventures. Stewart Aitchison

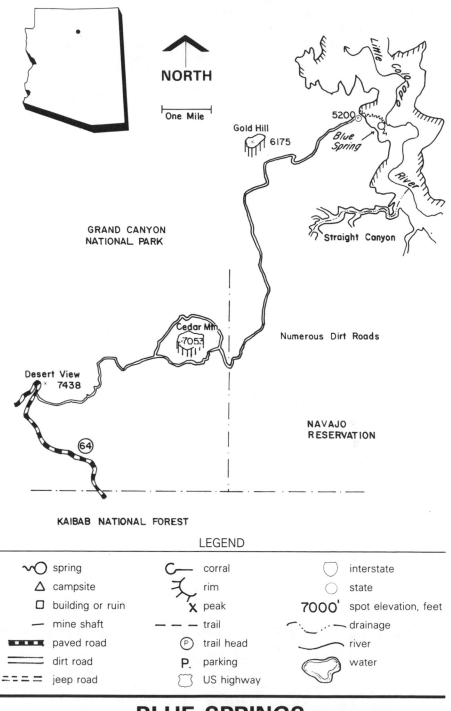

NORTH

One Mile

GRAND CANYON
NATIONAL PARK

Gold Hill
× 6175

5200

Blue
Spring

Little Colorado

River

Straight Canyon

Numerous Dirt Roads

Cedar Mtn.
× 7053

Desert View
× 7438

64

NAVAJO
RESERVATION

KAIBAB NATIONAL FOREST

LEGEND

∼⊙	spring	Ⅽ―	corral	⬡	interstate
△	campsite	rim	⬭	state
☐	building or ruin	✗	peak	7000'	spot elevation, feet
—	mine shaft	– – –	trail	⌒‥‥‥	drainage
▪▪▪▪	paved road	Ⓟ	trail head		river
=	dirt road	P.	parking	⬭	water
= = =	jeep road	⬠	US highway		

BLUE SPRINGS HIKE 11

it varies from season to season and year to year. The best advice is to consult the topo map frequently, locate Gold Hill before leaving the pavement, and take the dirt roads that seem to head in that general direction. Eventually you will reach your destination.

Once you are on the rim of the Little Colorado River Gorge due east of Gold Hill, there are rock cairns marking the trailhead. The first couple of switchbacks are surprisingly like a horse trail, but then the trail degenerates into a scramble. Cairns and painted arrows direct you downward. There is at least one spot where most hikers will want to shed their packs and hand them down. A rope for belaying may be wise for one vertical section near the top. In the 1960s, a hiker from Flagstaff fell off this 'trail' and broke both her legs, so be forewarned.

Near the end of the trail, as you approach the unmistakable, final "Inner Gorge" formed by the Redwall Limestone, the trail once again appears to be a horse trail. But this good path of only several hundred yards ends at the brink of the final cliff. To reach the river, go upstream a few hundred feet to a break in the cliff. There is a good campsite on the far side of the Little Colorado, which is dry most of the year above the spring and thus no problem to cross. If, however, the river is in flood, think twice about crossing it or your silt-laden body may never be found.

The reward of this epic is, of course, Blue Springs. When the Little Colorado River is not in flood (usually flooding occurs during the spring run-off and then again after heavy summer thundershowers), Blue Springs gushes from the left (west) bank. The water has an incredible azure color due to mineralization, and as it rushes out of the rock, the water actually fizzes because it is so highly charged with carbon dioxide gas.— *Stewart Aitchison* □

HIKE 12 *RED BUTTE*

General description: A round-trip day hike near the Grand Canyon.
General location: Ten miles south of the south rim of the Grand Canyon.
Maps: Red Butte 7.5-minute quad; Kaibab National Forest map.
Difficulty: Easy.
Length: One mile one way.
Elevation: 6,000 to 6,700 feet.
Special attractions: Unique view of the Grand Canyon, Coconino Plateau, and San Francisco Peaks.
Water: None.
Best season: April through November.
For more information: Tusayan Ranger District, P.O. Box 3088, Tusayan, AZ 86023; (602) 638-2443.
Permit: None.
Wilderness status: None—in fact, a uranium mine has been proposed for the area.

From Flagstaff, drive north on U.S. 180 to Valle (the junction with Arizona 64). This point may also be reached from Williams via Arizona 64. Drive north 11 miles to the Kaibab National Forest boundary and turn east on Forest Road 320. Here a sign describes Red Butte and its unique geology. Drive 1.5 miles

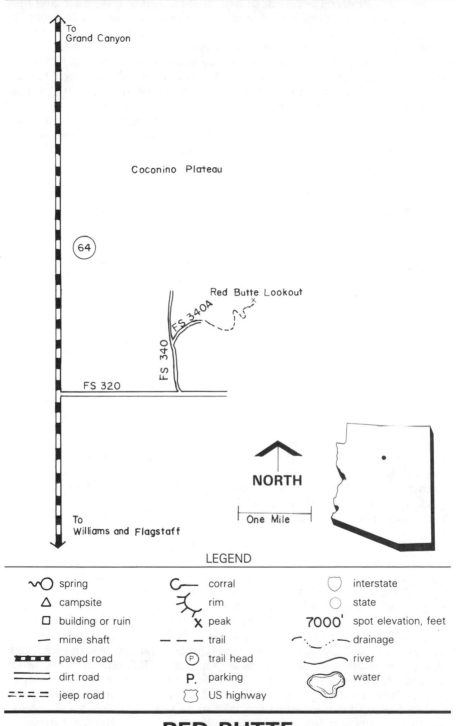

To
Grand Canyon

Coconino Plateau

(64)

Red Butte Lookout

FS 340A

FS 340

FS 320

To
Williams and Flagstaff

NORTH

One Mile

LEGEND

∿◯ spring	C⟍ corral	◯ interstate
△ campsite	🌿 rim	◯ state
▢ building or ruin	✗ peak	**7000'** spot elevation, feet
— mine shaft	– – – trail	⌒⋯⌒ drainage
▬▬▬ paved road	Ⓟ trail head	⌒⌒ river
═══ dirt road	P. parking	◯ water
= = = jeep road	⌂ US highway	

RED BUTTE HIKE 12

east and turn north on Forest Road 340. Drive about .8 mile north and turn east on Forest Road 340A, which ends at the marked trailhead in about .25 mile.

The well-constructed trail winds gradually up the pinyon-juniper forested southwestern slopes of the butte, climbing about seven hundred feet to the summit, which is your turnaround point. If it is manned, the Forest Service fire lookout offers hikers the best view. Be sure to ask the lookout's permission before climbing the single flight of stairs.

Red Butte is one of two surviving remnants of Mesozoic rock formations near the Grand Canyon. The upper walls of the Grand Canyon and the surface of the Coconino Plateau are composed of much older Paleozoic rocks. But only a few dozen miles to the east, these older rocks are buried under many thousands of feet of "middle aged" Mesozoic rocks. These rocks once covered the Grand Canyon area but have been completely eroded away, leaving only the small remnants at Red Butte and Cedar Mountain.—*Bruce Grubbs* □

HIKE 13 *RAINBOW BRIDGE TRAIL*

General description: Two- to three-day round-trip backpack trip.
General location: Just across the Utah line, east of Page, Arizona.
Maps: Navajo Mountain 15-minute, Chaiyahi Flat 7.5-minute USGS quads.
Difficulty: Moderate.
Length: Twelve miles one way.
Elevation: 6,300 to 3,700 feet.
Special attractions: Spectacular trail along the flanks of Navajo Mountain to Rainbow Bridge, one of the most beautiful natural bridges in the world.
Water: Cliff Canyon, Rainbow Bridge.
Best season: September-November, April-May.
For more information: Rainbow Bridge National Monument, P.O. Box 1507, Page, AZ 86040; (602) 645-2471.
Permit: Required. Obtain from Navajo Indian Reservation, P.O. Box 308, Window Rock, AZ 86515; (602)871-6647.
Wilderness status: None.

Leave U.S. 160 west of Cow Springs and turn north on Arizona 98. After about 12 miles, turn right (north) on the dirt Navajo Mountain Road. Stay on this road for about 33 miles to a main junction where the right fork goes to Navajo Mountain School. Take the left fork (there may be a sign for Rainbow Bridge Trail or Rainbow Lodge) about 6.5 miles to the road end at the ruins of Rainbow Lodge. There may be signs at the numerous minor forks in this road; it helps to have the Chaiyahi Flat map. Hide all valuables and securely lock your vehicle. There have been recent reports of vandalism at this trailhead.

The Rainbow Bridge Trail is the classic approach to Rainbow Bridge National Monument, and was the easiest route before the flooding of Glen Canyon by Lake Powell. Although the trail is only 12 miles long one way, the terrain is rugged enough that many parties take more than two days for the round trip, though it is certainly possible to do the trip in two. Rainbow Bridge is only the crowning glory of the trip. The walk in through enchanted glens of stone with the majestic dome of Navajo Mountain rising above is reward enough in itself.

From the site of Rainbow Lodge (a former commercial lodge and the beginning of guided pack trips to the Bridge), follow an old jeep trail northwest about a hundred yards, after which the trail contours west along the pinyon-juniper covered slope. After less than a mile it crosses First Canyon, the first of several canyon crossings as the trail skirts the rugged slopes of Navajo Mountain. About 4 miles from the trailhead it reaches a pass at the head of Cliff Canyon, then rapidly descends a steep talus slope to the bed of the canyon.

About 2 miles farther there is a spring in the bed which offers seasonal water along with a number of possible campsites. After another mile in Cliff Canyon the trail turns north and climbs over Redbud Pass (actually a joint, or crack, in the Navajo Sandstone) to Redbud Creek. The trail then follows Redbud Creek to Bridge Canyon. Hikers round a left turn in the canyon and suddenly the bridge and the end of the hike are visible. Old Echo Camp, used by commercial pack trips for many years before the creation of Lake Powell, offers camping possibilities just before entering the National Monument itself, and serves as the turnaround point of this hike.

Although Glen Canyon Dam sometimes backs water under the bridge (the subject of a long and bitter controversy, finally settled by the U.S. Supreme Court, over artificially flooding a National Monument), the boat dock was fortunately kept out of sight of the bridge. When waterborne tourists are absent, hikers can get a feel for the remoteness of this area before development of the dam and Lake Powell.

As shown on the Navajo Mountain map, another, longer trail skirts the north slopes of Navajo Mountain. This trail is much less used than the Rainbow Lodge Trail, and offers access to the labyrinth of redrock canyons flanking the mountain.—*Bruce Grubbs* □

Although Rainbow Bridge is located in Utah, the described hike begins in Arizona and traverses some of the most fantastic sandstone canyon country anywhere. In the background is snow-covered Navajo Mountain, a volcanic laccolith reaching over 10,000 feet above sea level. Bruce Grubbs

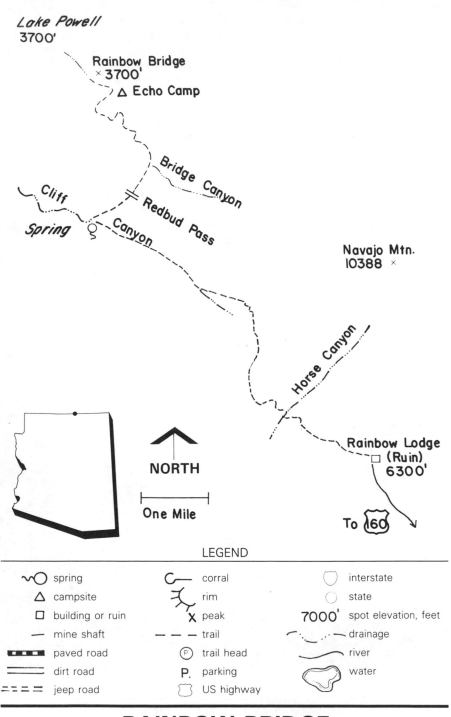

Lake Powell
3700'

Rainbow Bridge
× 3700'
△ Echo Camp

Bridge Canyon

Cliff

Redbud Pass

Spring

Canyon

Navajo Mtn.
10388 ×

Horse Canyon

NORTH

One Mile

Rainbow Lodge
□ (Ruin)
6300'

To 160

LEGEND

∿○	spring	C—	corral	◯	interstate
△	campsite	⊰	rim	◯	state
□	building or ruin	X	peak	7000'	spot elevation, feet
—	mine shaft	– – –	trail	⌒⋯⋯	drainage
▪▪▪▪	paved road	Ⓟ	trail head	⌒⌒	river
═══	dirt road	P.	parking	◯	water
≡≡≡	jeep road	◯	US highway		

RAINBOW BRIDGE HIKE 13

HIKE 14 *KEET SEEL*

General description: An overnight round-trip backpack to Arizona's largest cliff dwelling.

General location: Fifteen miles west of Kayenta.

Maps: Boot Mesa 15-minute, Betatakin Ruin 7.5-minute USGS quads.

Difficulty: Easy.

Length: Eight miles one way.

Elevation: 7,000 to 6,300 feet.

Special attractions: Very well preserved Anasazi cliff dwellings, beautiful sandstone canyon, an opportunity to experience the Navajo Reservation.

Water availability: Seasonal water that should be considered polluted by livestock. Carry your own.

Best season: Trail is only open from Memorial Day through Labor Day.

For more information: Navajo National Monument, HC 63 Box 3, Tonalea, AZ 86044; (602) 672-2366.

Permit: A permit is required from Navajo National Monument; reservations are recommended and can be made up to two months in advance.

Wilderness status: None.

The ruins, drawings, and artifacts of The Ancient Ones are common across northeastern Arizona. One of the most spectacular Anasazi villages is the 160-room cliff dwelling known as Keet Seel.

Keet Seel is a Navajo phrase meaning "broken pieces of pottery." As you

The prehistoric Anasazi Indians lived in northern Arizona from about the time of Christ until the fourteenth century. During this 1,300-year span only the last century saw extensive use of cliff houses such as this one, known today as Keet Seel. Earlier Anasazi lived in pit houses, which were partially subterranean huts, or in mud-and-stone pueblos. Stewart Aitchison

hike up the canyon bottom, potshards litter the sand. From the mid-tenth century to the late thirteenth century, several hundred people occupied Tsegi Canyon and its tributary, Keet Seel, and built several cliff dwellings. Here they grew corn, beans, and squash, tended turkeys, and molded exquisite pottery painted with geometric and animal designs. Then in the late 1200s, the people began to leave. What caused the abandonment—drought, disease, war, or over-population—is uncertain.

Even without reaching Keet Seel Ruin, this hike is worthwhile just for the sheer beauty of the canyon. Most of the route traverses Navajo land, so it is not uncommon to encounter small flocks of sheep and goats or perhaps glimpse a Navajo riding his horse to or from his hogan or traditional home.

Except for a short, steep, sandy stretch near the trailhead, the trail is mainly level and simply follows the canyon bottom. High walls of Navajo and Kayenta sandstones stand guard over the creek bed. As the trail meanders up the canyon, you pass plants typical of the plateau country—four-wing saltbush, big sagebrush, virgin's bower, Mormon tea, rabbitbrush, snakewood, pinyon pine, and juniper. You may also notice potshards, worked stone, or other artifacts of the Anasazi sticking out of the sandy trail. Please enjoy these treasures and leave them for future visitors.

It is necessary to obtain a permit from the park service at Navajo National Monument.

To reach the trailhead, turn off U.S. 163 onto Arizona 564 about 20 miles southwest of Kayenta. Drive 10 miles to Navajo National Monument and pick up your permit. The park rangers will tell you how to locate the trailhead and where to park your car.

At Keet Seel Ruin there is a primitive campground for overnight hikers but no water. Any water that you may find along the way is highly suspect and should only be used if you can treat it properly.—*Stewart Aitchison* □

HIKE 15 *WHITE HOUSE RUIN*

General description: A short round-trip day hike to one of the Southwest's most striking cliff dwellings.
General location: Seven miles east of Chinle.
Maps: Canyon del Muerto 15-minute USGS quad.
Difficulty: Easy.
Length: 1.25 miles one way.
Elevation: 6,000 to 5,500 feet.
Special attractions: Cliff dwellings, incredible sandstone canyons, and glimpses of Navajo Reservation life.
Best season: Anytime, although spring run-off and summer flooding occasionally make the crossing of Chinle Creek impossible.
For more information: Canyon de Chelly National Monument, Box 588, Chinle, AZ 86503; (602) 674-5436.
Permit: None required but you must stay on the trail.
  Wilderness status: None.

This is the only trail in Canyon de Chelly National Monument that you may

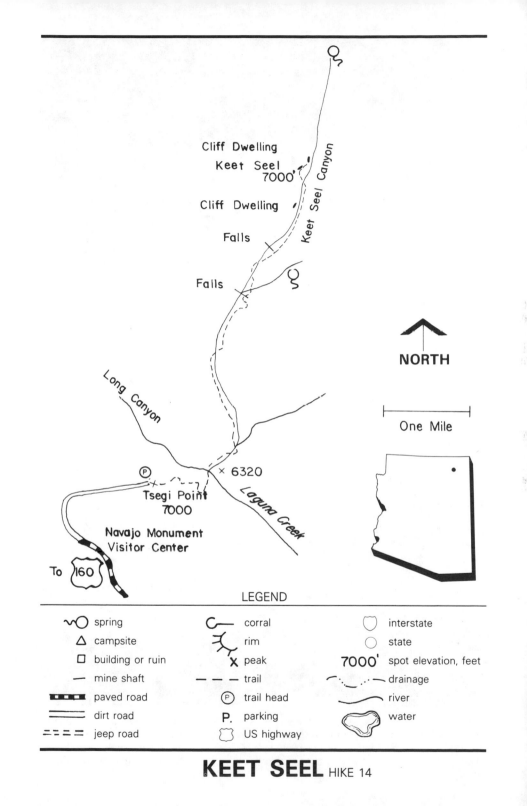

Cliff Dwelling
Keet Seel
7000'

Cliff Dwelling

Falls

Falls

Keet Seel Canyon

Long Canyon

NORTH

One Mile

P

× 6320

Tsegi Point
7000

Laguna Creek

Navajo Monument
Visitor Center

To 160

LEGEND

∿◯	spring	C—	corral	◯	interstate	
△	campsite	🔱	rim	◯	state	
☐	building or ruin	X	peak	**7000'**	spot elevation, feet	
—	mine shaft	– – –	trail	⌇	drainage	
▪▪▪▪	paved road	Ⓟ	trail head	⌇	river	
═══	dirt road	P.	parking	⬭	water	
= = =	jeep road	🛡	US highway			

KEET SEEL HIKE 14

White House Ruin in Canyon de Chelly is a well-preserved Anasazi site. Above the ruin are long, black streaks of desert varnish staining the sandstone cliff. Desert varnish, or patina, is a surface deposit of manganese or iron oxide. It usually forms where water periodically washes down the cliff, but the exact processes involved are still poorly understood. Bruce Grubbs

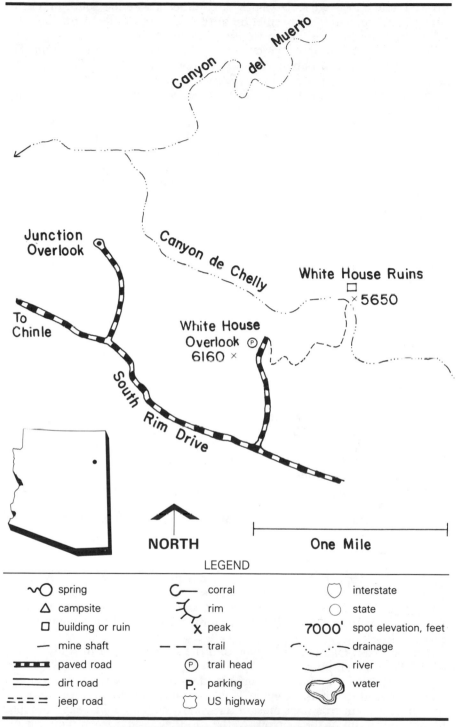

Canyon del Muerto

Junction
Overlook

Canyon de Chelly

White House Ruins
□
× 5650

To
Chinle

White House
Overlook Ⓟ
6160 ×

South Rim Drive

NORTH

One Mile

LEGEND

∿◯	spring	Ͼ⌐	corral	◯	interstate
△	campsite	⅄	rim	◯	state
□	building or ruin	X	peak	7000'	spot elevation, feet
—	mine shaft	– – –	trail	⌒⋅⋅⋅⌒	drainage
▪▬▪▬	paved road	Ⓟ	trail head	⌒⌒	river
═══	dirt road	P.	parking	⬭	water
≡≡≡≡	jeep road	⬠	US highway		

WHITE HOUSE RUIN HIKE 15

hike without a local guide. To reach the trailhead, take the South Rim drive from the monument visitor center on the east side of Chinle. After about 6.4 miles, turn left into the White House Overlook parking lot.

The trail begins about 150 yards to your right as you face the canyon. The trail switchbacks down about 500 vertical feet to the canyon floor opposite and just upstream from White House Ruin, named after the white plaster walls of the upper portion of the ruin. Plan twice as much time to return to the rim as it took you to descend.

This ruin, which is your turnaround point, consists of rooms built in the cave and a multi-storied masonry pueblo below. Access to the cave was by ladders from the rooftops of the lower pueblo. Perhaps fifty or more people lived in this village from approximately 1040 A.D. to 1275 A.D. They planted maize, squash, and beans along the canyon bottom much like the Navajo people do today, and they gathered wild fruits and nuts and hunted rabbits.— *Stewart Aitchison* □

HIKE 16 *EAST POCKET*

General description: A round-trip day hike into the Red Rock-Secret Mountain Wilderness Area.
General location: About mid-way through Oak Creek Canyon; about 9 miles north of Sedona on U.S. 89A.
Maps: Wilson Mountain 7.5-minute, Munds Park 7.5-minute USGS quads; Coconino National Forest map.
Difficulty: Easy.
Length: 2.5 miles to East Pocket Fire Lookout.
Elevation: 5,160 to 7,200 feet.
Special attractions: Splendid views of Oak Creek Canyon and surrounding Red Rock-Secret Mountain Wilderness Area; solitude.
Water availabilty: None once you leave Oak Creek.
Best season: Spring and fall. Crossing Oak Creek may be impossible during spring runoff.
For more information: Sedona Ranger District, P.O. Box 300, Sedona, AZ 86336; (602) 282-4119.
Permit: None.

Although the upper switchbacks of this trail are visible from one of Arizona's busiest (albeit spectacular) highways, it is rarely hiked. The majority of the 2.5 million annual visitors to Oak Creek Canyon seem to prefer to enjoy the canyon either from their autos or by sipping a few cool ones down by the creek.

For the hiker, Oak Creek Canyon and the surrounding rim country offer a variety of adventures.

In the 1870s, '80s, and '90s, homesteaders began to settle in the canyon. Since travel through the canyon was hampered by thick vegetation and numerous stream crossings, most of these early settlers built trails from their homes to the rim of the canyon. At the top they would leave their wagons and only bring their livestock and supplies down the trail.

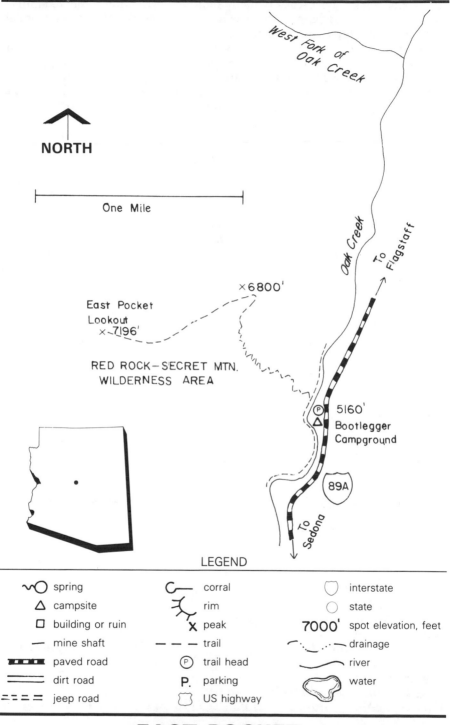

NORTH

One Mile

West Fork of Oak Creek

Oak Creek

To Flagstaff

×6800'

East Pocket
Lookout
×7196'

RED ROCK—SECRET MTN.
WILDERNESS AREA

P
5160'
△ Bootlegger
Campground

89A

To Sedona

LEGEND

ᵔ◯ spring	⊂— corral		◯ interstate
△ campsite	⋎ rim		◯ state
☐ building or ruin	✗ peak		7000' spot elevation, feet
— mine shaft	– – – trail		⌒···⌒ drainage
▰▰▰ paved road	Ⓟ trail head		⌒ river
═══ dirt road	P. parking		◌ water
≈≈≈ jeep road	⬡ US highway		

EAST POCKET HIKE 16

The East Pocket Trail was originally built as a cattle trail to move animals up to the ponderosa pine forest beyond the rim. In the 1930s, the Civilian Conservation Corps improved the trail.

To locate the trailhead, park at the Bootlegger Campground, which is about 9 miles north of Sedona on U.S. 89A. During the spring and fall this campground is closed but you can park along the highway. Walk through the campground and descend the steep bank to Oak Creek. Unless the creek is unusually high, you can find stepping stones that allow you to cross with dry feet.

On the west side of the creek, a definite trail runs parallel to the stream. Depending on exactly where you crossed, the East Pocket Trail will branch off this trail either a few hundred feet upstream or downstream. Don't be fooled by faint game paths leading uphill. The East Pocket Trail is a clearly defined trail marked by a Forest Service sign where it begins its upward climb to the rim, and it marks one of Arizona's newest (1984) designated wilderness areas, the Red Rock-Secret Mountain Wilderness Area.

The ascent to the rim takes you through a thick stand of chaparral vegetation.

The common plants include scrub live oak, mountain mahogany, silk-tassel bush, and manzanita. Banana and narrow-leaf yucca along with agave and prickly pear cactus make a formidable barrier to off-trail walking. Once on top, the vegetation makes a dramatic change to ponderosa pine forest with alligator-bark juniper and Gambel's oak along the forest edge.

Side-blotched, tree, and fence lizards are common in the chaparral, as are rufous-sided towhees. Gray-collared chipmunks, Steller's jays, and even black bears roam the pine forest.

At the rim, follow the remainder of the trail west to the East Pocket Fire Lookout, your turnaround point. Watch for faint tree blazes marking the way along the rim.

There are great views off the rim into Oak Creek Canyon, to the north of the San Francisco Peaks, and to the south into the Verde Valley. Hardy explorers may be able to find an exciting climbing route to the north into the West Fork of Oak Creek.—*Stewart Aitchison*

HIKE 17   *JACK'S CANYON*

General description: A round-trip day hike in Munds Mountain Wilderness Area.
General location: About a mile east of Oak Creek Village.
Maps: Munds Mountain 7.5-minute quad; Coconino National Forest map.
Difficulty: Moderate.
Length: About 7 miles one way.
Elevation: 4,200 to 6,400 feet.
Special attractions: A walk up a rough canyon, fine views of lower Oak Creek.
Water availability: None.
Best season: March through November.
For more information: Sedona Ranger District, P.O. Box 300, Sedona, AZ 86336; (602) 282-4119.
Permit: None.

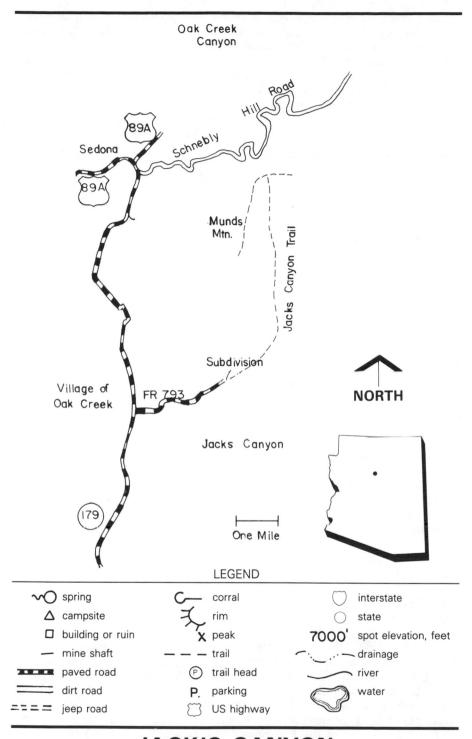

Oak Creek
Canyon

Hill Road

89A

Sedona

Schnebly

89A

Munds
Mtn.

Jacks Canyon Trail

Subdivision

Village of
Oak Creek

FR 793

NORTH

Jacks Canyon

One Mile

179

LEGEND

∿○	spring	C—	corral	◯	interstate
△	campsite	rim		○	state
▢	building or ruin	X	peak	7000'	spot elevation, feet
—	mine shaft	– – –	trail		drainage
▪▪▪▪	paved road	Ⓟ	trail head		river
	dirt road	P.	parking		water
= = = =	jeep road	⛉	US highway		

JACK'S CANYON HIKE 17

Take Arizona 179 to the village of Oak Creek (south of Sedona), and turn east on Jacks Canyon Road (Forest Road 793). Stay on Forest Road 793, which becomes dirt. The road ends in a subdivision. Park at the cattleguard at the entrance to this subdivision. The Jacks Canyon Trail begins as a jeep trail forking right just before this cattleguard. The jeep trail ends at Jacks Canyon Tank about 1.5 miles from the main road (also the Wilderness boundary). Forest Trail 55 continues up the canyon approximately 4 miles to the saddle between Munds Mountain and the Mogollon Rim. Trail 55 turns right and climbs a short distance to the Rim. Trail 77 goes left from the saddle and climbs to the gentle summit of Munds Mountain. From either of these points, return the way you came.

The entire saddle area offers fine views of lower Oak Creek Canyon and the Schnebly Hill area. The trail begins in typical chaparral scrub, consisting mainly of scrub oak, mountain mahogany, and manzanita. The higher parts of Jacks Canyon support a pinyon-juniper forest woodland while Munds Mountain is topped by ponderosa pine.—*Bruce Grubbs* □

HIKE 18 *SECRET MOUNTAIN*

General description: An overnight round-trip backpack into the heart of the Red Rock-Secret Mountain Wilderness Area.
General location: Ten miles northwest of Sedona.
Maps: Loy Butte 7.5-minute, Wilson Mtn. 7.5-minute USGS quads; Coconino National Forest map.
Difficulty: Moderate.
Length: Five miles to the top of Secret Mountain; an additional 1-3 miles for the best views.
Elevation: 4,720 to 6,400 feet.
Special attractions: Great views of the Red Rock Country from the top of Secret Mountain; solitude.
Water availability: Small springs on summit of Secret Mountain; may be dry in late summer.
Best season: Spring, summer, fall.
For more information: Sedona Ranger District, P.O. Box 300, Sedona, AZ 86336; (602) 282-4119.
Permit: None.

To locate the trailhead, drive about 10 miles west of Sedona on U.S. 89A and then turn right onto Forest Road 525. Take the right fork after 2.7 miles and the left fork after 5.7 miles. There is a sign here that reads, "Loy Butte—4 miles." At 9.2 miles from the highway and just before you cross a tree-lined wash, there is a small Forest Service sign on your right marking the Loy Canyon Trail. There is a parking area across the road to your left.

The Loy Canyon Trail will take you to the saddle connecting Secret Mountain and the main Mogollon Rim. From the saddle, the Secret Mountain Trail wanders out along the summit of the mountain through a ponderosa pine forest with exciting views of the Red Rock Country and the Verde Valley.

The trail begins in desert scrub consisting of catclaw acacia, Arizona cypress,

Yuccas are occasionally mistaken for cactus but are really members of the lily family. This is a banana yucca, so called because of its large, edible fruit. The Southwestern Indians, past and present, used the yucca plant for food, fiber, beverage, soap, and even as a laxative. Stewart Aitchison.

shrub live oak, narrowleaf and banana yucca, beargrass, and prickly pear cactus. The trail soon begins to follow a usually dry wash and the vegetation becomes more dense; alligator-bark juniper, mock orange, Virginia creeper, Arizona grape, and manzanita appear.

About .75 mile from the trailhead, you will see several small cliff dwellings in the alcove to the west.

These were built by the Sinaquans, a prehistoric agrarian people that occupied the Red Rock Country during the twelfth and thirteenth centuries.

As you continue up the trail, plants more typical of the forested rim area make their appearance; these include ponderosa pine, Douglas fir, white fir, buckbrush, cliffrose, and Gambel's oak. At about mile 3.5, the trail begins to switchback up through chaparral vegetation. You pass from the red Supai Formation, through the buff, cross-bedded Coconino Sandstone, and then contour through the gray Kaibab Limestone.

At the head of Loy Canyon, you reach the saddle connecting Secret Mountain with the main plateau. The adventuresome can bushwack down into the upper reaches of Secret Canyon. Most hikers, though, will prefer heading south along the trail out to viewpoints on Secret Mountain. Along the way you will pass several small tanks that generally contain water and the remains of Secret Cabin, where there is a small spring.

In the 1870s, Samuel Loy and his son James homesteaded in Loy Canyon. Unfortunately a drought during the 1880s forced them to relocate. During the late 1800s, this area was used by outlaws as a hideout. One story relates how horse rustlers brought stolen horses to the top of Secret Mountain, changed their brands, then took them to Utah, Colorado, or New Mexico to be sold.—*Stewart Aitchison* □

What is the secret of Secret Mountain? One legend says outlaws stayed at this old cabin atop the mountain, while another legend says Mormon polygamists hid out here in the 1880s. Stewart Aitchison.

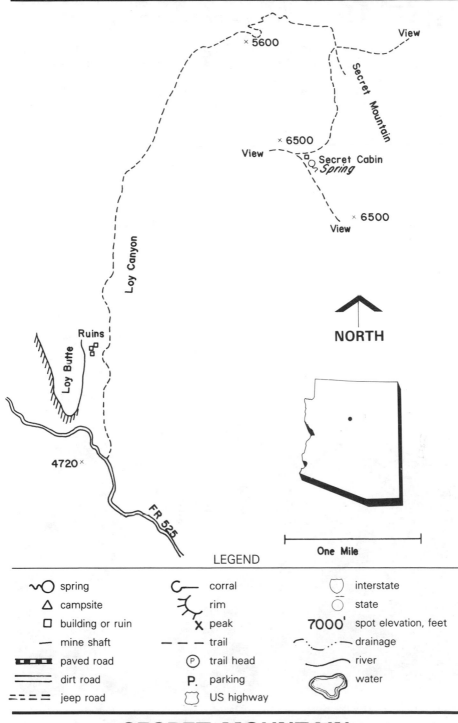

5600

View

Secret Mountain

6500
View

Secret Cabin
Spring

6500
View

Loy Canyon

Ruins

Loy Butte

4720

FR 525

NORTH

One Mile

LEGEND

∿○	spring	⌐	corral	⬡	interstate
△	campsite	⅄	rim	○	state
☐	building or ruin	X	peak	7000'	spot elevation, feet
—	mine shaft	– – –	trail	⌐⌐⌐	drainage
▪▪▪▪▪	paved road	Ⓟ	trail head	∿	river
══	dirt road	P.	parking	⬮	water
= = =	jeep road	⬠	US highway		

SECRET MOUNTAIN HIKE 18

General description: Two-to-three-day loop backpack through the Sycamore Canyon Wilderness and the Red Rock-Secret Mountain Wilderness areas.
General location: Twelve miles north of Cottonwood.
Maps: Loy Butte 7.5-minute, Sycamore Point 7.5-minute, Clarkdale 7.5-minute USGS quads; Coconino National Forest map.
Difficulty: Moderate.
Length: About 21 miles round trip.
Elevation: 4,300 to 6,400 feet.
Special attractions: Red rock canyons; solitude; wildlife.
Water availability: Seasonal water in Sycamore Creek and Mooney (Spring) Creek.
Best season: Spring and fall.
For more information: Sedona Ranger District, P.O. Box 300, Sedona, AZ 86336; (602) 282-4119.

Taylor Cabin deep in the Sycamore Canyon Wilderness is unique in that its back wall is a sandstone cliff. According to legend, somewhere nearby is a lost Spanish gold mine. The entrance to the mine is supposedly marked by a large meteorite. Stewart Aitchison.

Permits: None.

This two-to-three-day backpack takes you into two of the most beautiful areas of northern Arizona, the Sycamore Canyon Wilderness Area and the Red Rock-Secret Mountain Wilderness Area.

To find the trailhead, drive northeast out of Cottonwood toward Sedona on U.S. 89A. About 9 miles from Cottonwood turn left onto Forest Road 525. In 2.7 miles take the left fork, Forest Road 525C. Follow this road to its end at Sycamore Pass, a distance of about 12 miles.

The trail begins here among the red Supai and tan Coconino sandstone cliffs and is rocky as it descends from the pass into the Sycamore Wilderness Area and skirts through a pinyon-juniper woodland. It is easy to follow since it appears to have been a jeep road prior to becoming a foot trail. In about 5 miles the trail reaches the Sycamore Creek bed, which is usually dry although isolated pools may exist. After another .5 mile, you intersect the Sycamore Basin Trail coming from the southwest wilderness boundary. Check your topo map often, since the trail junction is not signed. Continue northeast, parallelling Sycamore Creek.

In about 3 miles you will come to Taylor Cabin, a cowboy line shack built in 1931. In the front wall are the carved brands of four ranches which have used it. Also are the names of the stone masons who built the cabin, Despain and Porter. The cabin is a designated National Historic Site. There are often pools of water in the creek bed near the cabin but these, too, can dry up by the end of summer.

Wildlife is abundant in the canyon. Tracks of javelina, mule deer, whitetail deer, and ringtail cats can be found. Rock squirrels and pack rats live around the cabin.

Look for black or brown hairs stuck on the rough edges of Forest Service trail signs such as this one in the Sycamore Canyon Wilderness Area. Black bear sometimes use these signs as scratching posts. Stewart Aitchison.

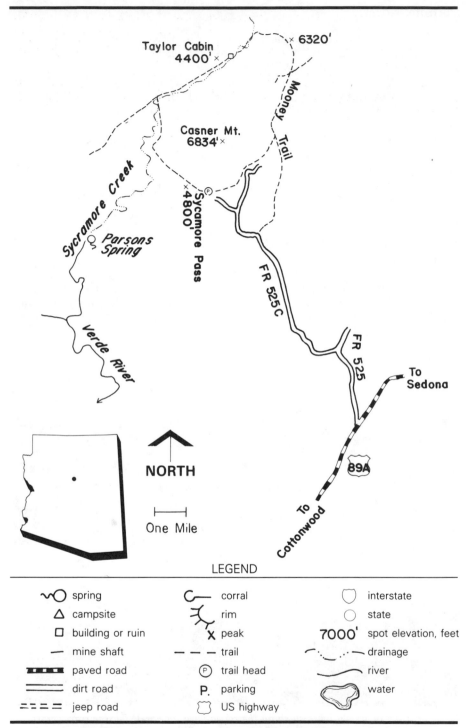

Taylor Cabin
4400' ×   × 6320'

Casner Mt.
6834' ×

Mooney Trail

Sycamore Creek

Parsons
Spring

× Sycamore Pass
4800'

Ⓟ

FR 525 C

FR 525

Verde River

To
Sedona

89A

To
Cottonwood

NORTH

⊢————⊣
One Mile

LEGEND

∿◯	spring	C—	corral	◯	interstate
△	campsite	⅄	rim	◯	state
▢	building or ruin	X	peak	7000'	spot elevation, feet
—	mine shaft	– – –	trail	∼⋯∼	drainage
▰▰▰	paved road	Ⓟ	trail head	∼	river
═══	dirt road	P.	parking	◯	water
= = =	jeep road	⬡	US highway		

SYCAMORE PASS-MOONEY LOOP HIKE 19

The trail continues upstream from Taylor Cabin 2 miles and then forks. The left branch goes another mile before exiting the canyon and passing Ott Lake and Winter Cabin. Your route, however, follows the right fork and climbs 1,800 vertical feet within 2 miles to Buck Ridge.

At the ridge, the trail crosses an old jeep road which follows a power line. You can follow this old road south to Casner Mountain and eventually back to Sycamore Pass. This way back to your car is about 7 miles and offers spectacular views of the San Francisco Peaks, Sycamore Canyon, the Verde Valley, and the Red Rock country.

Another alternative is to cross Buck Ridge and drop into Mooney Canyon via the fairly good horse trail. About .5 mile after reaching the canyon floor, the trail crosses the dry creek west to east. Here is a lovely grotto and arch carved into the Supai Sandstone. Javelina are common in this area, too, where the thick chaparral vegetation provides cover and one of their favorite foods, prickly pear cactus, is abundant.

After about 4.5 miles from Buck Ridge, the trail becomes fainter and confused by cow paths. Don't fret—just continue down the canyon on the most definite path until the canyon opens up, where you will be within a few hundred feet to the west of the jeep road shown on the Loy Butte quad. To return to Sycamore Pass either follow the jeep road 525B to Black Tank and then walk up 525C, or else contour around to the southwest until you encounter road 525C. This second choice can be brushy but does save you a couple of miles.—*Stewart Aitchison* □

HIKE 20 *GERONIMO SPRINGS*

General description: A round-trip day hike or overnight trip in the remote upper end of the Sycamore Canyon Wilderness Area.
General location: About 17 miles southeast of Flagstaff.
Maps: Sycamore Point 7.5-minute USGS quad; Coconino National Forest map.
Difficulty: Moderate.
Length: Three miles one way.
Elevation: 6,800 to 5,200 feet.
Special attractions: Elk, black bear, mule deer; solitude; a deep, narrow canyon.
Water availability: Several springs.
Best season: Late spring through fall.
For more information: Flagstaff Ranger District, 1100 N. Beaver, Flagstaff, AZ; (602) 527-7450.
Permit: None.

To reach the beginning of this delightful hike, drive out of Flagstaff on the Turkey Butte Road (Forest Road 231) on the west end of town on Old Route 66. The Turkey Butte Road turns off just west of the Kit Carson Trailer Park. About 18 miles from the highway, take Forest Road 538 for 4.5 miles. Then turn right onto 538E. Follow this to its end in 1.5 mile. The maze of roads near the canyon is confusing, but by using the Forest Service map in conjunction with the topo quad you should be able to stay on the right course.

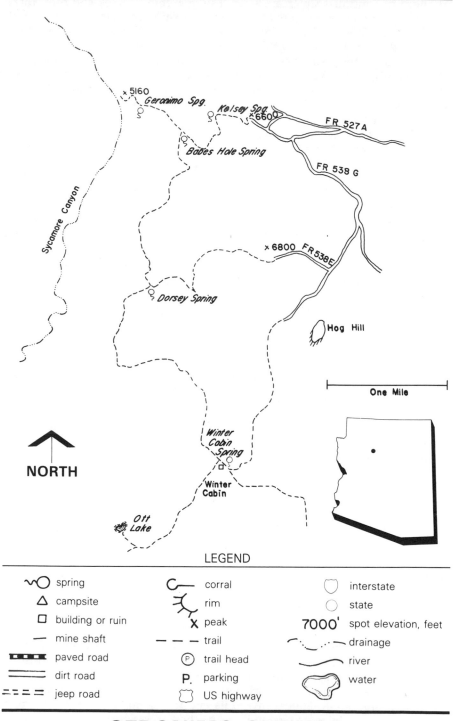

x 5160
Geronimo Spg.

Kelsey Spg.
x 6600
FR 527 A

Babes Hole Spring

FR 538 G

Sycamore Canyon

x 6800 FR 538 E

Dorsey Spring

Hog Hill

One Mile

NORTH

Winter
Cabin
Spring

Winter
Cabin

Ott
Lake

LEGEND

∿○	spring	C⊃	corral	◠	interstate
△	campsite	⋎	rim	○	state
▢	building or ruin	X	peak	**7000'**	spot elevation, feet
—	mine shaft	– – –	trail	⌐⋯	drainage
▄▪▪▪	paved road	Ⓟ	trail head	∼	river
═══	dirt road	**P.**	parking	⬠	water
= = =	jeep road	⬠	US highway		

GERONIMO SPRINGS HIKE 20

Generally this route is passable to two-wheel drive vehicles with good clearance, but do not attempt it if there has been a lot of rain recently.

From the end of the road, the signed trail takes off downhill through a ponderosa pine forest. Wild turkey and deer are common. In a little over a mile you reach Dorsey Spring, which is permanent. The trail forks here. The left branch contours south toward Winter Cabin and other trails leading to Sycamore Canyon. (The ruin of Winter Cabin is the unnamed black square at the spring shown in the extreme northeast corner of section 14 on the USGS quad.) The right fork is your route.

Another 1.5 miles through the pines brings you to Babes Hole Spring, another dependable water source. The last .5 mile of trail to Geronimo Springs, your turnaround point, descends rapidly to the canyon floor.

Watch for elk in this area, as well as black bear scat and tracks.—*Stewart Aitchison* □

HIKE 21 *WET BEAVER CREEK*

General description: A round-trip day hike or easy overnight into The Wet Beaver Wilderness Area.
General location: About 2.5 miles east of the Sedona exit on Interstate 17.
Maps: Casner Butte 7.5-minute USGS quad; Coconino National Forest map.
Difficulty: Easy.
Length: About 3 miles one way (to junction of Long Canyon).
Elevation: 3,800 to 4,100 feet.
Special attractions: Spectacular, rugged canyon; permanent stream.
Water: Permanent stream.
Best season: April through November.
For more information: Beaver Creek Ranger District, Rimrock, AZ 86335; (602) 567-4501.
Permit: None.

From Interstate 17 in the Verde Valley, take the Sedona Exit (Arizona 179) but turn east onto Forest Road 618. Drive about 2 miles and turn east at the sign for Wet Beaver Creek. Park after .25 mile at the trailhead. Trail 13, the Bell Trail, begins as an old jeep trail. After about 2 miles it becomes a foot trail, and just before this point the unsigned Apache Maid Trail climbs away from Wet Beaver Creek to the north. The Bell Trail continues to skirt the north side of the creek, following the running stream with its fine swimming holes and lush riparian vegetation (including poison ivy—beware!). After about a mile, there are several good campsites. At this point the Bell Trail crosses the creek to the south and climbs southeast to the canyon rim where there are fine views of the area. This makes a good turnaround point for the hike.—*Bruce Grubbs* □

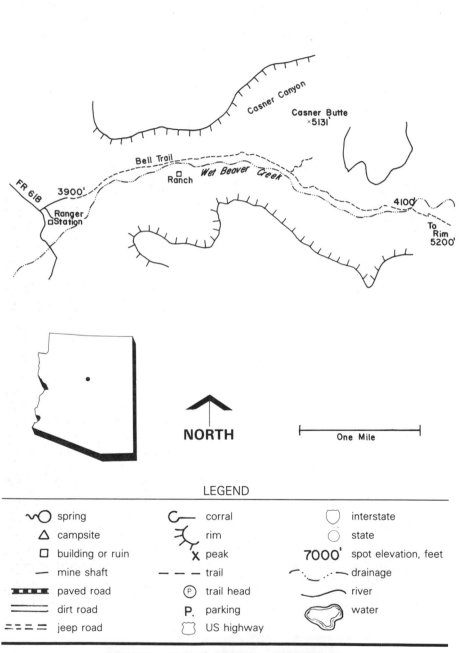

Casner Canyon

Casner Butte
×5131'

Bell Trail

FR 618

3900'

Ranch

Wet Beaver Creek

Ranger
Station

4100'

To
Rim
5200'

NORTH

One Mile

LEGEND

⌒○	spring	C⌒	corral	⬡	interstate	
△	campsite		rim	�	state	
□	building or ruin	X	peak	7000'	spot elevation, feet	
—	mine shaft	– – –	trail	⌒‥‥	drainage	
▪▪▪▪	paved road	Ⓟ	trail head	⌒⌒	river	
═══	dirt road	P.	parking	⬭	water	
= = =	jeep road	🛡	US highway			

WET BEAVER CREEK HIKE 21

HIKE 22 *WEST CLEAR CREEK*

General description: Two-day or longer loop backpack (and swim) through the West Clear Creek Wilderness Area.

General location: Twelve miles east of Camp Verde.

Maps: Calloway Butte 7.5-minute, Buckhorn Mountain 7.5-minute USGS quads; Coconino National Forest map.

Difficulty: Moderate to difficult (cross-country).

Length: Nine miles round trip.

Elevation: 6,650 to 5,200 feet.

Special attractions: A permanent clear water stream with great swimming holes.

Water availability: Clear stream and springs; best to purify.

Best season: Summer and early fall.

For more information: Long Valley Ranger District, P.O. Box 68, Happy Jack, AZ 86024; (602) 774-7289.

Permit: None.

Hiking often turns into swimming in West Clear Creek. Some backpackers pack their gear in a heavyweight plastic bag, which traps enough air to buoy a backpack. Other hikers bring along a small vinyl raft or inner tube. But beware of flash floods, particularly during the thunderstorm season of July and August. Stewart Aitchison

Overlooking the West Clear Creek Wilderness, this Parry agave is in full bloom. Agaves are also called century plants because they wait many years, usually from eight to thirty years, before sending up a stalk and flowering. After this one blooming, the plant dies. The fermented pulp of a Mexican species of agave produces the fiery beverage tequila. Stewart Aitchison

This backpack is challenging because the "trail" is mostly the creek and there are several places where you must swim to continue down the canyon. But it is well worth every effort. Just as you think the canyon with its soaring Coconino Sandstone walls couldn't be lovelier, you round the corner and the cold trout stream jumps off into a crystal clear pool so deep that you can barely discern the bottom.

There are a number of ways into and out of the canyon. This hike description is for the central, more remote section. To find the trailhead, turn off of the General Crook Trail (Forest Highway 9) onto Forest Road 144. This is about 3 miles from the junction of the General Crook Trail and Arizona 87. After about 2 miles, turn left onto Forest Service Route 149. Proceed to Route 142 and turn left. About 4.5 miles later you will see New Tank on your right. Park here.

Follow Forest Road 142B, which is the jeep trail leading northward from the east side of New Tank. In about 2 miles you will come to a fence on the rim of West Clear Creek. Just to your left is a small gate which leads you to a short, steep trail to the canyon floor.

If you are feeling lazy, this idyllic spot can be your goal. Lush vegetation lines the stream; ponderosa pine, Douglas fir, and white fir cover the canyon walls. In their cool shade, Virginia creeper, New Mexico locust, bigtooth maple, and Arizona grape thrive. Crayfish and trout lurk in the watery shadows, trying to avoid becoming a meal for a nearby belted kingfisher. A mule deer crashes through the brush while a broad-tailed hummingbird whirs to a brilliant scarlet penstemon flowering along the creek.

If you can tear yourself away, more spectacular sites await downstream.

You must follow the topographic map carefully or else the sinuous winding of the canyon will disorient you and finding the correct exit will be difficult.

The 5 miles or so to your exit point can be traveled in a strenuous day, but there are so many wonderful swimming spots that two or even three days is not unreasonable. Most of your walking will be in water calf- or knee-deep, but there are several spots where swimming will be necessary. This hike should not be undertaken in spring or early summer when high runoff and cold water could mean hypothermia. And during the thunderstorm season of July and August, flash floods may occur, so exercise caution.

Some hikers have solved the "pool crossing" problem by bringing lightweight one-person rafts to put their packs in. Others put their belongings in waterproof rubber bags which in turn fit inside their packs. Enough air is trapped inside the bags to make the backpacks float reasonably well. But even in August the water can be chilly.

As you travel downstream, you will notice that the character of the canyon changes. In places the stream is clogged with massive gray basalt boulders, a particularly tedious part of the trip as you attempt to hop from rock to rock. Other stretches of the canyon are enclosed by soaring sandstone cliffs and the stream spreads out across a sandstone bed nearly as flat as a sidewalk.

About 4 miles downstream from the entry point, you pass through a .75-mile relatively straight stretch of canyon trending to the northwest. You then arrive at another falls and a long pool that must be swum. After this the stream turns to the south (more or less). Your exit route is located about .3 mile farther, just before the canyon narrows again and the stream begins a series of steep drops. But if you have the time, slip off your pack and continue downstream

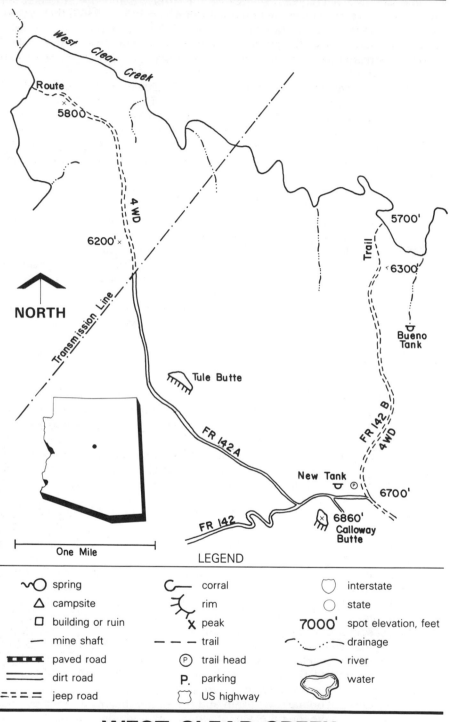

West Clear Creek

Route
5800
4 WD
6200'
Transmission Line

NORTH

5700'
Trail
6300'
Bueno Tank

Tule Butte

FR 142A

FR 142 B
4WD

New Tank
6700'
6860'
Calloway Butte

FR 142

One Mile

LEGEND

ᗧ◯	spring	ᑕ	corral	◯	interstate	
△	campsite	⑂	rim	◯	state	
☐	building or ruin	X	peak	**7000'**	spot elevation, feet	
—	mine shaft	– – –	trail		drainage	
▬▬▬	paved road	Ⓟ	trail head		river	
═══	dirt road	P.	parking		water	
≡≡≡	jeep road	⬡	US highway			

WEST CLEAR CREEK HIKE 22

another .25 mile. Here you will find some of the deepest and longest pools of the entire canyon, one of which is 100 yards long with sheer cliffs plunging into the water.

Back at the exit route, you will notice several faint game trails leading upward, and the Coconino National Forest map indicates the presence of Trail 40. However, I have never been able to locate Trail 40, so just head uphill through the chaparral. It's only a few hundred yards to the rim and if you choose your route carefully, you can avoid most of the prickly, scratchy vegetation. At the rim, walk easterly a few hundred yards and you will cross the jeep track that leads 4 miles back to New Tank.

If you have two four-wheel drive vehicles, you can also arrange a shuttle by leaving one of them closer to the rim, saving you as much as 6 miles of walking.—*Stewart Aitchison*

HIKE 23 *CHEVELON CANYON*

General description: A two- or three-day round-trip backpack in a wooded canyon.
General location: Forty miles south of Winslow.
Maps: Chevelon Crossing 7.5-minute USGS quad; Apache-Sitgreaves National Forest map.
Difficulty: Moderate.
Length: About 10 miles one way.
Elevation: 6,300 to 7,000 feet.
Special attractions: Beaver are common in Chevelon Creek.

Upper Chevelon Canyon is wide enough that hiking along the creek bank is feasible. Downstream, however, the canyon narrows and swimming becomes necessary. Poison ivy and the thorny New Mexican locust are also common along the creek, so watch your step. Stewart Aitchison

Water availability: Chevelon Creek is permanent.
Best season: Spring through fall.
For more information: Chevelon Ranger District, 1520 W. Third Street, Winslow, AZ, 86047; (602) 289-3381.
Permit: None.
Wilderness status: None.

This is a delightful backpack into a forested canyon containing one of Arizona's rarest resources, a permanent trout stream. Drive south out of Winslow on Arizona 99 for approximately 38 miles to Chevelon Crossing and campground.

From here, it is about a 10-mile hike upstream to Chevelon Canyon Lake, a manmade reservoir which is your turnaround point. Along the way are beaver ponds, swimming holes, and grassy campsites amid ponderosa pine, cottonwood, locust, and other riparian species. There is no formal trail but it is possible to walk along the canyon floor, following game and livestock paths, without too many stream crossings. Elk and deer are common.

Exploration downstream is also possible but somewhat more difficult. The canyon narrows, and more time is necessary to cross or even sometimes swim the creek. One time we attempted to hike all the way to Chevelon Creek's confluence with the Little Colorado River, but were turned back about halfway there by a massive barrier of floating logs. It was impossible to walk across them or around them, and the canyon walls at that spot were unclimbable.

In 1851, Captain Lorenzo Sitgreaves wrote that the stream received its name from a trapper called Chevalon who died after eating some poisonous root along its bank. Poison hemlock does grow along the creek, and may well have been the culprit.—*Stewart Aitchison* □

HIKE 24 *AUBINEAU-REESE CANYON*

General description: A loop day hike in the Kachina Peaks Wilderness Area.
General location: North slopes of the San Francisco Peaks, north of Flagstaff.
Maps: Humphreys Peak 7.5-minute, White Horse Hills 7.5-minute USGS quads; Coconino National Forest map.
Difficulty: Moderate.
Length: About 8 miles.
Elevation: 8,250 to 10,400 feet.
Special attractions: Alpine forest of fir and aspen, views of north slopes of Humphreys Peak.
Water availability: Snow early season, otherwise none.
Best season: June through October.
For more information: Elden Ranger District, 2519 E. 7th Avenue, Flagstaff, AZ 86001; (602) 527-7470.
Permit: None.

Drive about 18 miles north of Flagstaff on U.S. 180, then turn east onto Forest Road 151. After approximately 1.5 miles, turn left onto Forest Road 418. In about 4 miles, turn right (south) at the Aubineau Trail sign and onto

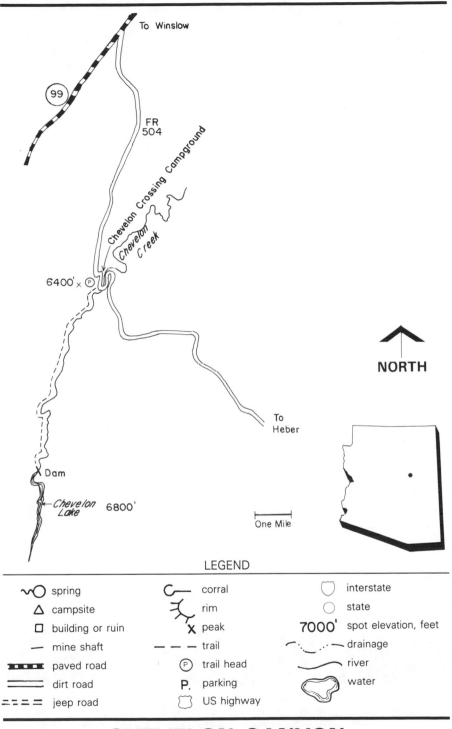

To Winslow

99

FR
504

Chevelon Crossing Campground

Chevelon Creek

6400' × Ⓟ

NORTH

To
Heber

✕ Dam

Chevelon
Lake

6800'

⊢———⊣
One Mile

LEGEND

∿⊙	spring	ℂ—	corral	⬡	interstate
△	campsite	⋎	rim	◯	state
☐	building or ruin	✕	peak	**7000'**	spot elevation, feet
—	mine shaft	– – –	trail	⌁	drainage
▰▰▰	paved road	Ⓟ	trail head	∿	river
═══	dirt road	**P.**	parking	◌	water
= = = =	jeep road	⬯	US highway		

CHEVELON CANYON HIKE 23

a rough road, which leads .25 mile to Reese Tanks (low clearance vehicles can be left on F.R. 418).

Just south (uphill) from the stock tanks, follow a badly eroded jeep trail up the gradual slope. In about .5 mile, the old road forks; take the right fork (the left fork leads to the Reese Trail). After several hundred yards the Aubineau Trail forks right from the road and contours west into Aubineau Canyon. Do not continue on the jeep trail—it dead ends.

The trail continues up the bed of the canyon for approximately 2 miles. At the lower end, the forest is primarily ponderosa pine. Watch for especially large, old trees, a sign that the area has never been heavily logged. Gradually the ponderosas thin out as aspen, limber pine, and then fir and spruce take over at increasing elevations. The trail ends at the Aubineau Canyon road at 10,400 feet in a large meadow with a fine view of the north ridge of Humphreys Peak.

Although it would be possible to climb from here to the summit, the Forest Service has forbidden off-trail hiking above timberline because of the fragile nature of the tundra and the existence of an endemic alpine plant, the San Francisco Peaks groundsel, which is threatened with extinction.

Note several unforested chutes running down into the meadow from the north ridge of Humphreys. These are active avalanche paths during the winter. There are enough large avalanches to keep the area at the end of the trail and about .25 mile down the canyon completely cleared of trees.

It is possible to make a loop trip by continuing east on the Abineau Canyon road about 2.5 miles to the Reese Trail. As you walk, you will first cross Reese Canyon, and then Bearjaw Canyon. About .5 mile past Bearjaw, watch for the unmarked trail dropping down the gentle slope to the north. Follow this

The higher slopes of the San Francisco Peaks comprise the Kachina Peaks Wilderness Area. A popular trail which begins at the Fairfield Snowbowl ski lodge climbs the highest summit, Humphreys Peak at 12,670 feet. The Aubineau-Reese Canyon loop described in this guide, will get you away from the crowds. Stewart Aitchison.

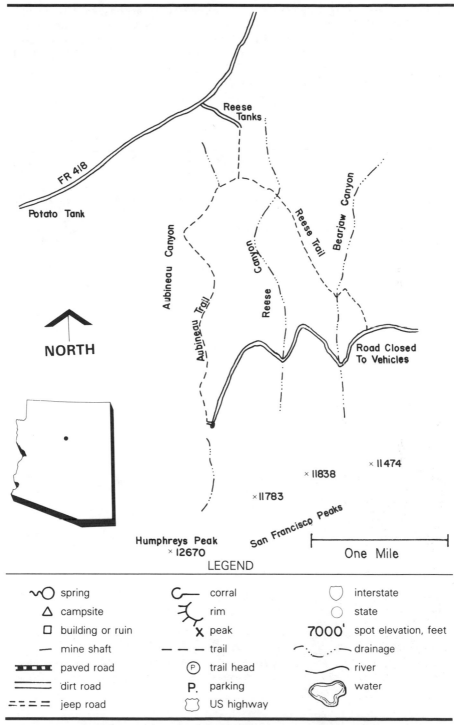

Reese
Tanks

FR 418

Potato Tank

Aubineau Canyon

Aubineau Trail

Reese Canyon

Reese Trail

Bearjaw Canyon

NORTH

Road Closed
To Vehicles

× 11474

× 11838

× 11783

San Francisco Peaks

Humphreys Peak
× 12670

One Mile

LEGEND

∿○	spring	⊂	corral	⬡	interstate	
△	campsite	〤	rim	○	state	
▢	building or ruin	X	peak	**7000'**	spot elevation, feet	
—	mine shaft	– – –	trail	⌁ ⋅⋅	drainage	
▰▰▰	paved road	Ⓟ	trail head	⌇	river	
═══	dirt road	**P.**	parking	⬭	water	
＝＝＝	jeep road	⬠	US highway			

AUBINEAU-REESE CANYON HIKE 24

trail as it continues down a gentle slope covered with aspens, then turns left and crosses Bearjaw Canyon. Occasional cairns mark the trail through a confusing maze of old logging roads as it continues northwest toward Reese Tanks. After crossing Reese Canyon, the trail ends at the old jeep trail mentioned above. Follow the road back to Reese Tanks and your vehicle.

The Aubineau Trail is a recent extension of an old jeep trail which climbed part-way up the canyon. The Reese Trail is an old sheepherder's trail which has recently been improved. Increasing hiker and horse traffic will probably keep both trails distinct. —*Bruce Grubbs* □

Near the top of Arizona, Humphreys Peak in the Kachina Peaks Wilderness Area—here shown on an early March hike and ski—averages more than two hundred inches of snow each winter. Stewart Aitchison

HIKE 25 *SLATE MOUNTAIN*

General description: A round-trip day hike in forest northwest of the San Francisco Peaks.
General location: Thirty miles north of Flagstaff.
Maps: Kendrick Peak 7.5-minute quad; Coconino National Forest map.
Difficulty: Easy.

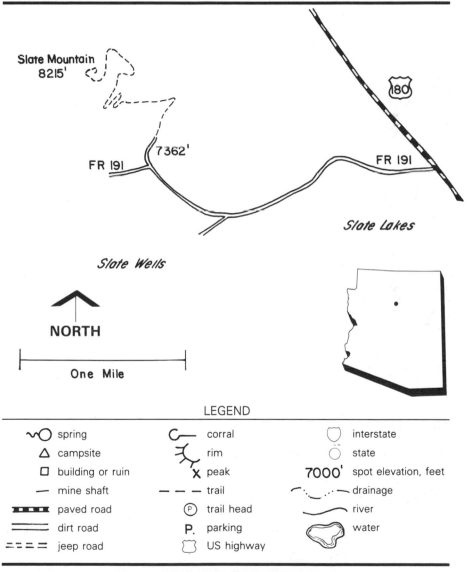

Slate Mountain
8215'

180

7362'

FR 191

FR 191

Slate Lakes

Slate Wells

NORTH

One Mile

LEGEND

∿⃝	spring	C—	corral	⃝	interstate
△	campsite	🜊	rim	○	state
☐	building or ruin	X	peak	**7000'**	spot elevation, feet
—	mine shaft	– – –	trail	⌢‥⌢‥	drainage
▪▪▪▪	paved road	Ⓟ	trail head	～	river
═══	dirt road	**P.**	parking	⬭	water
═ ═ ═	jeep road	⬠	US highway		

SLATE MOUNTAIN HIKE 25

Length: About 2 miles one way.
Elevation: 7,450 to 8,200 feet.
Special attractions: Pleasant and easy ascent to fine views of San Francisco volcanic field.
Water availability: None.
Best season: May through October.
For more information: Flagstaff Ranger District, 1100 N. Beaver Street, Flagstaff, AZ 86001; (602) 527-7450.
Permit: None.
Wilderness status: None.

Drive about 26 miles north of Flagstaff on U.S. 180, then turn west on Forest Road 191. The Slate Mountain trail is signed and is approximately 2 miles from the highway. Drivers of low clearance vehicles may wish to avoid the last .25 mile of road.

The trail is obvious and easy to follow, switchbacking up south slopes through pinyon-juniper woodland. Higher, the trail winds through ponderosa pine, then rounds the north side into Douglas fir. The view from the 8,215-foot summit, your turnaround point, is open and offers an expansive view of the northern slopes of the San Francisco Peaks and Kendrick Mountain, as well as Coconino Plateau.

Slate Mountain is an old cinder cone, one of several hundred located generally north of Flagstaff in the San Francisco volcanic field. The Slate Mountain Trail is actually an old road, now closed to vehicles, which was used to service a fire lookout. The tower, along with several others on the north end of the forest, has long since been torn down.—*Bruce Grubbs* □

HIKE 26 *LAVA RIVER CAVE*

General description: Round-trip day hike into a lava tube.
General location: Fifteen miles northwest of Flagstaff.
Maps: Coconino National Forest map.
Difficulty: Easy.
Length: Less than a mile round trip.
Elevation: 7,680 feet (no significant elevation change).
Special attractions: A unique geologic feature.
Water availability: None.
Best season: Spring through fall; winter, too, if you ski in.
For more information: Flagstaff Ranger District, 1100 N. Beaver Street, Flagstaff, AZ 86001; (602) 527-7450.
Permit: None.
Wilderness status: None.

This is a different kind of hike—you explore the inside of a lava flow. When the molten rock began to cool, the interior of the flow continued to move, leaving a tube or cave in its wake.

To find the Lava River Cave, drive north out of Flagstaff on Arizona 180 about 13.5 miles and then turn left onto Forest Road 245. In about 3 miles you will come to a T-intersection, where you turn left onto Forest Road 171. Go just over a mile and turn left, again, onto 171A. A few hundred feet later, the road ends at the mouth of the cave.

Be sure each person in your party has at least two lights. It can get very dark in a lava tube. A Coleman-style lantern is a great illuminator. You may want to wear a hard hat.

The cave is quite different from solution caverns found in limestone. It contains no stalactites, stalagmites, or confusing labyrinths or side tunnels. Instead, it is just a single dead-end tunnel with a fairly rounded ceiling and rocky floor, almost like a primordial subway.—*Stewart Aitchison* □

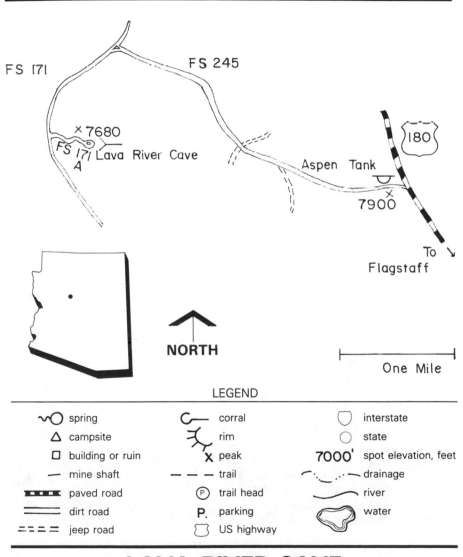

LEGEND

∿◯	spring	Ϲ—	corral	◯	interstate	
△	campsite	⅄	rim	◯	state	
▢	building or ruin	**X**	peak	**7000'**	spot elevation, feet	
—	mine shaft	— — —	trail		drainage	
▰▰▰▰	paved road	Ⓟ	trail head		river	
═══	dirt road	**P.**	parking		water	
═ ═ ═	jeep road	▢	US highway			

LAVA RIVER CAVE HIKE 26

HIKE 27 *KENDRICK MOUNTAIN*

General description: A round-trip day hike into Kendrick Mountain Wilderness Area.

General location: Twenty-five miles northwest of Flagstaff.

Maps: Kendrick Peak 7.5-minute USGS quad; Kaibab National Forest South map.

Difficulty: Moderate.

Length: Four miles one way.

Elevation: 8,000 to 10,400 feet.

Special attractions: Beautiful hike through alpine forest, superb views of San Francisco Peaks and the Coconino Plateau.

Water: Snow early season, otherwise none.

Best season: May through October.

For more information: Flagstaff Ranger District, 1100 N. Beaver Street, Flagstaff, AZ 86001; (602) 527-7450.

Permit: None.

Drive about 16 miles north from Flagstaff on U.S. 180, turn west onto Forest Road 193, and drive 3 miles west to Forest Road 171. Turn right (north) and drive about 3 miles to road 171A. This road ends at the signed trailhead in less than a mile.

The well-maintained trail climbs the south slopes of Kendrick Mountain. The lower part of the trail is a former jeep trail built to fight a fire on East Newman Hill many years ago. Higher, the trail switchbacks upward through stands of limber pine and aspen. Near the summit ridge, the forest changes

Typically cloudless nights make tentless camping a real possibility in Arizona, but carry at least a tarp just in case. This prime campsite is located near the top of Kendrick Peak. Bruce Grubbs

to that typical of Canada, with Engelmann spruce and Arizona corkbark fir. Just below the summit, the trail passes the old lookout cabin and the junction with the Bull Basin Trail. The final switchbacks lead to the summit cone and offer fine views to the south and east. A few yards from the lookout building, your turnaround point, the Pumpkin Center trail (see hike #28) branches off. If the lookout is home, he'll probably welcome the company. Just remember that the fire lookout is his home and be sure to ask before climbing.—*Bruce Grubbs* □

HIKE 28 *PUMPKIN CENTER*

General description: A round-trip day hike into Kendrick Mountain Wilderness Area.
General location: Thirty miles northwest of Flagstaff.
Maps: Kendrick Mountain 7.5-minute, Moritz Ridge 7.5- minute USGS quads; Kaibab National Forest South map.
Difficulty: Moderate.
Length: 4.5 miles one way.
Elevation: 7,200 to 10,400 feet.
Special attractions: Little-used trail with fine views en route.
Water availability: Snow in early season, otherwise none.
Best season: May through October.
For more information: Flagstaff Ranger District, 1100 N. Beaver Street, Flagstaff, AZ 86001; (602) 527-7450.
Permit: None.

Drive about 16 miles north from Flagstaff on U.S. 180, then turn west onto Forest Road 193. Drive 3 miles west to Forest Road 171, turn right (north), and drive about 6 miles to Pumpkin Center. A sign points out the trailhead.

The trail starts as an old logging road and climbs east up the side of Bull Basin Mesa for a little more than a mile, then becomes a foot trail and starts up the west ridge of Kendrick Mountain. You will pass the junction with the wilderness boundary trail which connects to the Bull Basin Trail (see hike #29). The Pumpkin Trail continues up the ridge, steeply at times, while the forest changes from ponderosa pine to limber pine and aspen, alpine meadows and Douglas fir, and finally Engelmann spruce and bristlecone pine near the summit. There are excellent views to the west from the meadows.

The summit is the logical turnaround point on this hike, but you can also make this trek a loop by continuing down the Bull Basin Trail (see hike #29).— *Bruce Grubbs* □

HIKE 29 *BULL BASIN*

General description: A round-trip day hike in the Kendrick Mountain Wilderness Area.
General location: Forty miles northwest of Flagstaff.

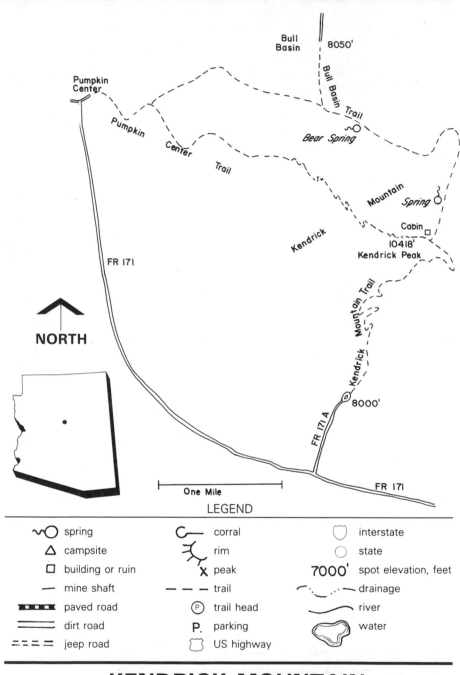

LEGEND

∽◯	spring	⊂—	corral	◌	interstate
△	campsite	⋎	rim	◯	state
▢	building or ruin	✗	peak	**7000'**	spot elevation, feet
—	mine shaft	– – –	trail	⌒‥⌒	drainage
▪▪▪▪	paved road	Ⓟ	trail head	⌒⌒	river
══	dirt road	P.	parking	◯	water
≡≡≡	jeep road	⌂	US highway		

NORTH

One Mile

KENDRICK MOUNTAIN HIKE 27
PUMPKIN CENTER HIKE 28
BULL BASIN HIKE 29

Maps: Kendrick Mountain 7.5-minute. Moritz Ridge 7.5-minute USGS quads; Kaibab National Forest South map.
Difficulty: Moderate.
Length: 4.5 miles one way.
Elevation: 7,050 to 10,400 feet.
Special attractions: Little-used trail, loop with Pumpkin Center Trail.
Water availability: Bear Spring, not shown on maps.
Best season: May through October.
For more information: Flagstaff Ranger District, 1100 N. Beaver Street, Flagstaff, AZ 86001; (602) 527-7450.
Permit: None.

Drive about 16 miles north from Flagstaff on U.S. 180, then turn west onto Forest Road 193. Drive 3 miles west to Forest Road 171, turn right (north), and drive about 9 miles. Turn north (right) on Forest Road 144. Drive 1.25 miles, turn east (right) on Forest Road 90 and follow this road about 6 miles to the signed trailhead.

From the signed trailhead, the Bull Basin Trail climbs gradually up the north slopes of Kendrick Mountain through mixed pine, fir, and aspen. About .5 mile from the trailhead, you will reach the signed junction with the wilderness boundary trail. The Bull Basin Trail continues up the slope past Bear Spring and then ascends through fine fir forest to a saddle and open meadows bordered with aspen. Now the trail turns south and climbs to the old lookout cabin on the east ridge of Kendrick Mountain, where it joins the Kendrick Lookout Trail in an open meadow with hundred-mile views to the south. Continue on the Lookout Trail to reach the summit and the junction with the Pumpkin Center Trail. Then return the way you came, or return via the Pumpkin Center Trail to make this a loop hike.—*Bruce Grubbs* □

HIKE 30 *WHITE HORSE HILLS*

General description: A round-trip day hike north of the San Francisco Peaks.
General location: Twenty miles north of Flagstaff.
Maps: White Horse Hills 7.5-minute USGS quad; Coconino National Forest map.
Difficulty: Easy.
Length: About a mile one way.
Elevation: 8,500 to 9,050 feet.
Special attractions: Close and spectacular views of Humphreys Peak.
Water availability: None.
Best season: May through November.
For more information: Flagstaff Ranger District, 1100 N. Beaver Street, Flagstaff, AZ 86001; (602) 527-7450.
Permit: None.
Wilderness status: None.

Drive about 18 miles north of Flagstaff on U.S. 180, then turn east onto Forest Road 151 (North Hart Prairie Road). Drive east about 2 miles through beautiful stands of aspen and pine. Turn left (east) onto Forest Road 418. Drive east 2 miles to a large meadow with a stock tank and a cattleguard. This is Potato Tank Meadow.

The trail starts a few yards west at the highest point in the road. It is a former jeep trail which has been closed by the Forest Service. It ascends north to a saddle. From here it climbs along the slope to a higher saddle and forks. The left fork leads to the highest point of the White Horse Hills while the right fork leads to the east summit, which is only slightly lower. Both summits are turnaround points for this hike, both are approximately the same distance from the trailhead, and either offers excellent views of the northwest slopes of the San Francisco Peaks as well as the volcanic field to the north and west.

The White Horse Hills seem to be an old, badly eroded cinder cone, but there are some outcrops of Kaibab Limestone on the highest summit. This rock forms the general surface of the surrounding plateau, except where it is locally covered by cinders and lava. Perhaps large chunks of limestone were blasted loose during the eruption of the White Horse Hills and were carried up the vent to lodge near the surface.—*Bruce Grubbs* □

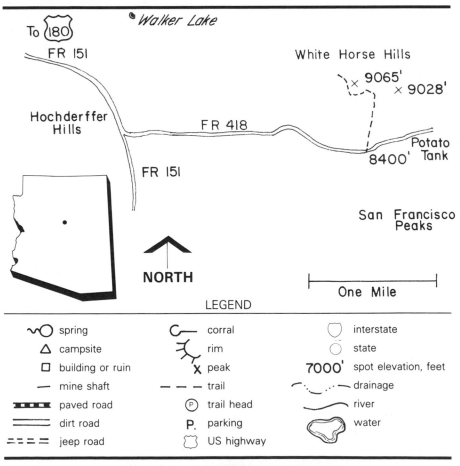

WHITE HORSE HILLS HIKE 30

HIKE 31 *MOUNT ELDEN*

General description: A round-trip day hike in Flagstaff.
General location: East Flagstaff.
Maps: Flagstaff West 7.5-minute USGS quad; Coconino National Forest map.
Difficulty: Moderate.
Length: Three miles one way.
Elevation: 6,900 to 9,300 feet.
Water availability: None.
Best season: April through November.
For more information: Elden Ranger District, 2519 E. 7th Avenue, Flagstaff, AZ 86001; (602) 527-7470.
Permit: None.
Wilderness status: None.

Drive to the Elden Ranger Station in east Flagstaff. The marked turnoff to the ranger station is located along Santa Fe Avenue just north of the Flagstaff Mall. Park at the signed trailhead.

The Elden Trail runs north along the east slopes of Mount Elden for about a mile before suddenly turning east and switchbacking steeply to the summit and your turnaround point. The forest is open and the views of east Flagstaff and the surrounding plateau are spectacular.

Little hint remains of the beautiful fir-aspen forest which thickly covered the summit before the Radio Fire in 1977. The fire was man-caused and started at the south base of the mountain on a hot and windy day. It spread explosively up the south slopes, across the summit area, and down the north and northeast slopes, and was only stopped at U.S. 89 after several days. Today one can clearly see the aspen beginning to prepare the way for a new fir forest, several hundred years in the future.

The summit area is reached by a road from the west, and a fire lookout and numerous radio towers crowd the top.—*Bruce Grubbs* □

HIKE 32 *STRAWBERRY CRATER*

General description: A short day hike in the Strawberry Crater Wilderness Area.
General location: Twenty miles northeast of Flagstaff.
Maps: Strawberry Crater 7.5-minute USGS quad; Coconino National Forest map.
Difficulty: Easy (cross-country).
Length: About .5 mile to rim of Strawberry Crater (no trail).
Elevation: 6,000 to 6,500 feet.
Special attractions: Recent and dramatic volcanic activity, rich archaeology.
Water availability: None.
Best season: Spring and fall.
For more information: Elden Ranger District, 2519 E. 7th Avenue, Flagstaff, AZ 86001; (602) 527-7470; Wupatki National Monument (for archaeological

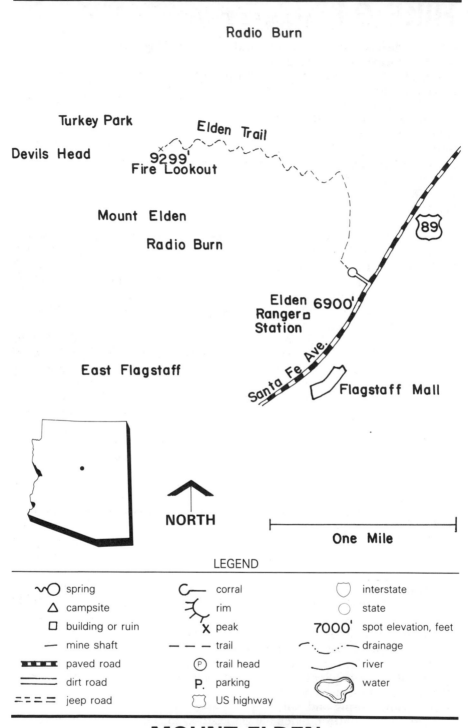

Radio Burn

Turkey Park

Elden Trail

Devils Head

9299'
Fire Lookout

89

Mount Elden

Radio Burn

Elden 6900'
Ranger
Station

Santa Fe Ave.

East Flagstaff

Flagstaff Mall

NORTH

One Mile

LEGEND

∿◯	spring	↶	corral	◯	interstate
△	campsite	⋎	rim	◯	state
◻	building or ruin	X	peak	7000'	spot elevation, feet
—	mine shaft	– – –	trail	⌣	drainage
▪▪▪▪	paved road	Ⓟ	trail head	⌒	river
═══	dirt road	P.	parking	◌	water
= = = =	jeep road	⌂	US highway		

MOUNT ELDEN HIKE 31

information), HC33, Box 444A, Flagstaff, AZ 86001; (602) 527-7040; Sunset Crater National Monument (for geologic information), Route 3, Box 149, Flagstaff, AZ 86001; (602) 527-7042.
Permit: None.

To reach the area, drive 12 miles north from Flagstaff on U.S. 89, then turn east (right) on the road to Sunset Crater (Forest Road 545, paved). Drive through the monument to Painted Desert Vista, about 8 miles from U.S. 89. From here you can hike cross-country north and northeast into the cinder dune area of the Strawberry Crater Wilderness.

Another route begins about 15 miles north of Flagstaff on U.S. 89. Turn east (right) on Forest Road 546, an unimproved dirt road. Drive about 3.5 miles to the junction with Forest Road 779, and take this road about 2 miles to the west base of Strawberry Crater. Do not drive off the road—you can easily get stuck in the deep, loose cinders.

It is an easy cross-country walk to your turnaround point, the top of Strawberry Crater from the west base. The volcanic terrain is loose and jagged, and there is no trail. However, the view from the summit ridge is more than worth the climb. You can see the San Francisco Peaks to the southwest and the colorful Painted Desert and the Navajo Indian Reservation to the northeast.

Hiking around the base of Strawberry Crater and across the lava flow and cinder field is easier, although sturdy boots are valuable and gaitors may help keep pesky cinders out of your socks.

During the springtime and the summer monsoon months, many different flowers, grasses, and shrubs bloom, and wildlife is visible much of the year. A partial list of wildlife and vegetation commonly encountered on this hike includes mule deer, elk, coyote, several species of hawk, great horned owl, Townsend's solitaire, common flicker, plain titmouse, junco, western and mountain bluebird, one-seed juniper, pinyon pine, ponderosa pine, rubber rabbitbrush, Apache plume, desert olive, currant, phacelia, aster, California bricklebrush, skyrocket, and sand bluestem grass. One species, *Penstemon clutei*, is found only in this area.

The area was home to the prehistoric Sinagua Indians 700-900 years ago. Pit houses used for temporary shelter during farming and hunting activities are numerous, and unique terraced garden areas in the cinders are still recognizable today. Walled structures in near-perfect condition remain in some parts of the area, which seems to have been used seasonally for farming by people who lived in the large, more permanent structures of nearby Wupatki National Monument. A few pueblos in the area may have been occupied year-round, as the climate allowed.

A visit to Wupatki and Sunset Crater national monuments before your hike will provide excellent cultural and geologic background information, making your visit more interesting and rewarding. Please remember to hike with care so as not to disturb any archaeological artifacts you may encounter. These sites are protected by law so their cultural and historical significance may be preserved for future generations. These valuable resources are extremely important to scientists, and may be irrevocably changed by disturbance.—
John Nelson □

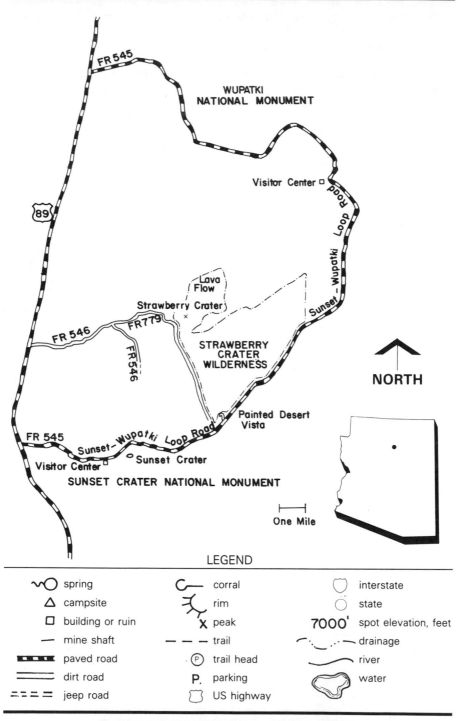

FR 545

WUPATKI
NATIONAL MONUMENT

Visitor Center □

Sunset – Wupatki Loop Road

89

Lava
Flow

Strawberry Crater ×

FR 546   FR 779

FR 546

STRAWBERRY
CRATER
WILDERNESS

NORTH

Painted Desert
Vista

FR 545   Sunset–Wupatki Loop Road

Visitor Center □   ○ Sunset Crater

SUNSET CRATER NATIONAL MONUMENT

One Mile

LEGEND

⌀○ spring	⊂ corral	⬡ interstate
△ campsite	⋔ rim	○ state
□ building or ruin	✗ peak	7000′ spot elevation, feet
— mine shaft	– – – trail	⌢‥⌢ drainage
▪▫▪▫ paved road	Ⓟ trail head	⌒ river
═══ dirt road	P. parking	⬯ water
═ ═ ═ jeep road	⬡ US highway	

STRAWBERRY CRATER HIKE 32

HIKE 33 *BILL WILLIAMS MOUNTAIN*

General description: A round-trip day hike on a forested volcano.

General location: About a mile west of Williams.

Maps: Bill Williams Mountain 15-minute USGS quad; Kaibab National Forest South map.

Difficulty: Moderate.

Length: Three miles one way.

Elevation: 6,900 to 9,250 feet.

Special attractions: Cool and shady walk up north-facing canyon, views of highcountry around Williams.

Water availability: None.

Best season: May through October.

For more information: Williams Ranger District, Rt.1, Box 142, Williams, AZ 86046; (602) 635-2633.

Permit: None.

Wilderness status: None.

From Williams, drive west on I-40 to the Camp Clover exit. Drive to Camp Clover (a Forest Service station) and park at the signed trailhead.

The trail ascends onto a bench covered with pinyon and juniper, then climbs into the cool, north-facing head of West Cataract Creek as the forest gives way to ponderosa pine, fir, and aspen. This drainage is part of the headwaters of Cataract Creek, which enters famous Havasu Canyon many miles to the north. The trail finally switchbacks up to end at the Bill Williams Road, which leads a short distance farther to the summit and your turnaround point. This trail is an excellent hike on a hot summer day.

The trail was built by the Forest Service for access to the fire tower on the summit before a road was built.—*Bruce Grubbs* □

HIKE 34 *PINE MOUNTAIN*

General description: Two-day loop hike in the Pine Mountain Wilderness Area.

General location: Twenty-five miles east of Cordes Junction.

Maps: Tule Mesa 7.5-minute USGS quad; Prescott National Forest map.

Difficulty: Moderate.

Length: About 17 miles.

Elevation: 5,200 to 6,800 feet.

Special attractions: Remote and little-hiked area, with excellent views of the wild parts of the Verde River and the Mazatzal Mountains.

Water availability: See description.

Best season: April through November.

For more information: Verde Ranger District, HC 62, Box 1100, Camp Verde, AZ 86322; (602) 567-4121.

Permit: None.

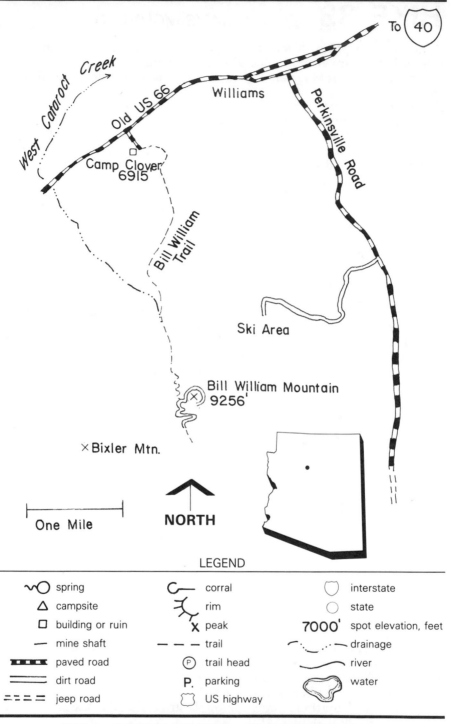

BILL WILLIAMS MOUNTAIN HIKE 33

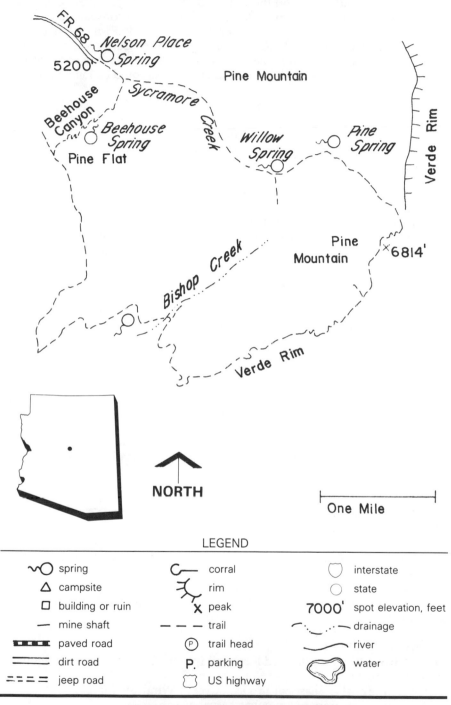

FR 68

Nelson Place
Spring

5200'

Pine Mountain

Beehouse
Canyon

Sycramore Creek

Beehouse
Spring

Pine Flat

Willow
Spring

Pine
Spring

Verde Rim

Bishop Creek

Pine
Mountain

×6814'

Verde Rim

NORTH

One Mile

LEGEND

spring	corral	interstate
△ campsite	rim	state
building or ruin	X peak	7000' spot elevation, feet
— mine shaft	— — — trail	drainage
paved road	(P) trail head	river
dirt road	P. parking	water
jeep road	US highway	

PINE MOUNTAIN HIKE 34

From I-17 north of Cordes Junction, take the Dugas Road exit and go east 25 miles to the road's end and the trailhead. This road (Forest Road 68) can be rough beyond Dugas. A high-clearance vehicle is recommended.

Pine Mountain is a small wilderness astride the Verde Rim offering super views of both the wild Verde River country south of Camp Verde and the northwestern Mazatzal Mountains. If it weren't for a powerline corridor just outside the Pine Mountain Wilderness, the two areas could be joined into one wilderness.

From the signed road end at Nelson Place Spring (featuring good camping and water), it is possible to complete a loop hike over the highest point in the wilderness, Pine Mountain, in one long day or two easier days.

Walk about .25 mile up the trail along Sycamore Creek, then turn south on the signed Beehouse Canyon trail (Forest Trail 165) which climbs a mile to the head of Beehouse Canyon. Here the trail meets the signed Pine Flat Trail (Forest Trail 165). Turn southeast (left) toward Pine Flat. The trail crosses Pine Flat, a fine stand of Ponderosa pines, and continues south into the South Prong of Sycamore Creek, then climbs to meet the Verde Rim Trail in a saddle. Turn east (left) on the signed Verde Rim Trail (Forest Trail 59) which contours around to Bishop Creek. Bishop Spring is located in the drainage west of Bishop Creek and should be reliable.

At Bishop Creek, a signed trail (Forest Trail 159) offers a shortcut back to Sycamore Creek and the road head. Take the right fork southeast (Forest Trail 161) about a mile to the edge of the Verde Rim. The trail now turns northeast and climbs along the rim toward Pine Mountain. Some sections may be brushy. About .75 mile south of Pine Mountain, you pass the signed junction with Forest Trail 14. Forest Trail 161 continues through a fine pine grove, then passes just below the summit of Pine Mountain. The summit itself is easy to reach, though there is no trail, and is open with excellent 360-degree views.

North of Pine Mountain, Forest Trail 161 descends steeply to a saddle at the head of Sycamore Creek and the junction with the Willow Spring Trail. Turn west (left) on this trail. About .5 mile further on, there is seasonal water and Willow Spring should be reliable. From here, it is an easy and pleasant walk along the trail down Sycamore Creek to the trailhead.—*Bruce Grubbs* □

HIKE 35 *DEER CREEK*

General description: Two- or three-day loop hike in the Mazatzal Wilderness Area.

General location: Twenty miles southwest of Payson.

Maps: Mazatzal Peak 7.5-minute USGS quad; USFS Mazatzal Wilderness map.

Difficulty: Moderate.

Length: About 16 miles.

Elevation: 3,550 to 6,000 feet.

Special attractions: Little-used loop trail into the head of a forested canyon below fine peaks.

Water availability: Seasonal in Deer Creek, Windsor Camp.

Best season: September-November, April-May.

For more information: Payson Ranger District, P.O. Box 100, Payson, AZ

85541; (602) 474-2269.
Permit: None.

The Deer Creek Trailhead is probably the easiest Mazatzal trailhead to reach. It is only a few yards off a paved highway, yet is not heavily used. From Arizona 87, just north of the junction with Arizona 188, turn west on Forest Road 492. Drive through the gate and park at the fork in the road.

Three trails start from this trailhead, all infrequently used. It is possible to use two of these trails as part of a fine overnight or three-day loop hike into the rugged and scenic country at the head of Deer Creek.

Follow the right fork in the road a few yards to the signed start of Deer Creek Trail (Forest Trail 45). The trail works its way north about .5 mile through desert grassland and drops into Deer Creek. It then follows the creek west through riparian growth of cottonwood and sycamore trees (the stream flows most of the year). After about 2 miles, the trail passes the creek's confluence with Bars Canyon. The trail becomes narrower and rougher, climbing along the south wall of the canyon. Over the next 3-4 miles the trail climbs steadily, finally entering a fine stand of ponderosa pine just before reaching the site of Chilson Camp (McGowan Camp on the wilderness map). This area of open meadows offers a number of possible campsites. There is normally water in the creek except during long dry periods.

Forest Trail 45 continues up the creek a short distance then climbs steeply out to the south, reaching the Mount Peeley road (Forest Road 201) a short distance from its end. It is possible to hike up the Divide Trail (Forest Trail 23) and explore the interesting country around Mount Peeley. It is also easy to hike cross-country up Mount Peeley from the north.

You can return to your car via Deer Creek or else return on Forest Trail 46 via the South Fork of Deer Creek.

Traces of the past are common in the Mazatzal Wilderness. This old Forest Service sign predates 1953, when the Crook National Forest was divided into the Tonto, Coronado, and Gila national forests. Bruce Grubbs

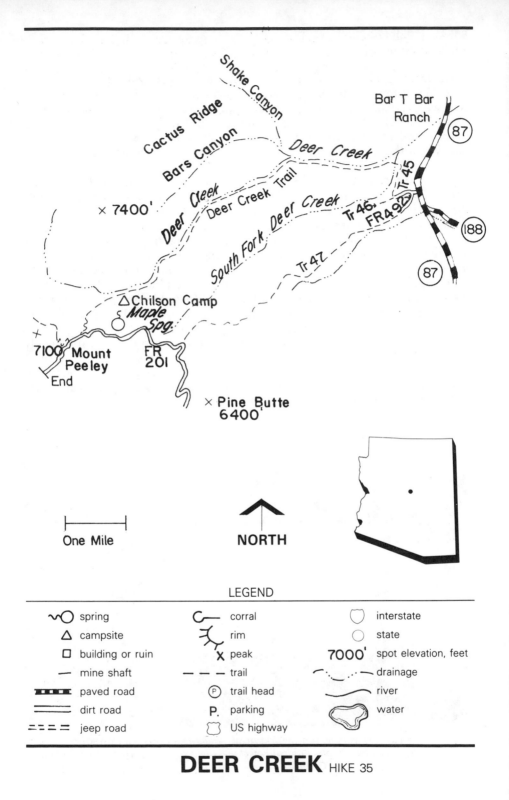

LEGEND

∿○	spring	C⊂	corral	⬡	interstate
△	campsite	⋉	rim	○	state
◻	building or ruin	X	peak	**7000'**	spot elevation, feet
—	mine shaft	– – –	trail	⌇	drainage
▬▬▬	paved road	Ⓟ	trail head	◠◡	river
═══	dirt road	**P.**	parking	◯	water
‗‗‗	jeep road	⬡	US highway		

One Mile

NORTH

DEER CREEK HIKE 35

Forest Trail 47 follows an especially scenic route. To do this, walk east from the end of Forest Trail 45 on the Mount Peeley road about 2 miles. Because the road is long and rough there is little traffic. Maple Spring, located just north of the road about a mile east of the Deer Creek Trail, is unsigned but may be a reliable water source. Except near the start where it passes through an old burn, the road stays on north-facing slopes shaded by fine stands of ponderosa pine and Douglas fir. About 2 miles from the Deer Creek Trail (Forest Trail 45), the road swings abruptly south out of the forest, and at this point Forest Trail 47 forks left (northeast).

The trail starts as a jeep trail which is closed after a short distance, and continues through tall pines, working its way northwest down the complex ridge system. About 3 miles from the Mount Peeley road, the trees finally give way to chaparral. The foot trail veers right from the old jeep trail, which ends at a mine, climbs over a small hill, then drops rapidly off the ridge to end at the trailhead. It is a pleasant 2-mile walk down the road to the fork near the highway.—*Bruce Grubbs* □

HIKE 36 *BARNHARDT-SHAKE TREE*

General description: Two- or three-day loop hike in the Mazatzal Wilderness Area.
General location: About 18 miles southwest of Payson.
Maps: Mazatzal Peak 7.5-minute; USFS Mazatzal Wilderness map.
Difficulty: Moderate.
Length: About 15 miles.
Elevation: 4,200 to 6,000 feet.
Water availability: At the trailhead, Chilson Spring, and Y Bar Tanks.
Special attractions: A fine sampler of the rugged terrain along the Mazatzal crest.
Best season: April through November.
For more information: Payson Ranger District, P.O. Box 100, Payson, AZ 85541; (602) 474-2269.
Permit: None.

From Arizona 87, turn west onto the dirt Barnhardt Road, which is located about 3 miles north of the junction with Arizona 188. Drive about 5.5 miles to the end of the road. There are three trails which start here: the Barnhardt Trail, the Shake Tree Trail, and the Rock Creek Trail.

Using the Barnhardt and Shake Tree trails, hikers can tackle a classic loop trip around Mazatzal Peak, the spectacular high point of the range. While most of the trails in the Mazatzals are rough and difficult to follow, these two trails were rebuilt by the Forest Service in the late 1960s and have been maintained since. They provide a good introduction to the characteristics of the range.

From the trailhead, follow the signed Barnhardt Trail as it climbs up into Barnhardt Canyon. There are good views of the permanent stream in Barnhardt as the canyon narrows. A series of switchbacks lead around the head of a sidecanyon; then the trail swings around a point into the upper basin of the Barnhardt drainage. It is worthwhile to walk out on this point; there are excellent views of upper Barnhardt Canyon and the precipitous east slopes of the range. The trail continues through heavy brush, the result of an old fire, past the signed turnoff to Castersen Seep (unreliable) and Sandy Saddle. It passes through some surviving stands of ponderosa pine before reaching Barnhardt Saddle and the junction with the Divide Trail at the head of the canyon.

The Mazatzal Mountains are heavily scarred by old and not-so-old wildfires. In much of Arizona's ponderosa pine country (areas lying at 6,500 feet or higher), ponderosa pine destroyed by fire are eventually replaced by new ponderosa pine. Lower, drier areas like the Mazatzals are not so favorable for ponderosa pine, however, and the burned forest is usually replaced by dense thickets of manzanita and scrub oak. One explanation for this difference is that mature pines are much more tolerant of heat and drought than pine seedlings and so can survive a climate which has become too dry now for seedlings to grow.

From Barnhardt Saddle, you can turn south (left) and start on the Divide Trail, but many hikers must take at least half a day to climb up Barnhardt Canyon and so may wish to camp first. Follow the Divide Trail to the right (northeast) about a mile to reach Chilson Camp, which offers numerous fine campsites in scattered pinyon-juniper, superb sunset views of the west face of Mazatzal Peak, and reliable water. (If the pipe is not running at the camp, you may have to follow it up the hill, above the Divide Trail, and do some spring maintenance). Chilson Camp has been used as a line camp by ranchers for many years, and the recent cleanup by the Forest Service has made it a pleasant place for hikers as well.

To continue the loop around Mazatzal Peak, either retrace your steps to Barnhardt Saddle and take the Divide Trail south or take the trail south from Chilson Camp past Brodie Seep. In either case, you will traverse below the west face of Mazatzal Peak to the Windsor Spring saddle, at the junction with the Shake Tree Trail. (Windsor Spring is not reliable.) The Shake Tree Trail descends rapidly into Y Bar Basin where there is reliable water at Y Bar Tanks (unmarked—see Mazatzal Peak quad), then climbs northwest to Shake Tree Saddle between Cactus Ridge and Mazatzal Peak. You can climb Mazatzal Peak via its southeast ridge from this saddle. From the saddle, the trail descends through a dense ponderosa forest and emerges on dry grassy slopes above Shake Tree Canyon, gradually descending to the Barnhardt trailhead.

Once the hangout of the Apache Indians, the Mazatzals have seen some mining activity but have been mainly used for grazing. These mountains have a reputation for rugged terrain which can quickly be verified by a short venture into one of their many canyons. Even today the long, rough trails seem to discourage most backpackers and only the Mazatzal Peak area is very popular.—*Bruce Grubbs* □

HIKE 37   *WILLOW SPRING—RED HILLS*

General description: A five- to seven-day loop hike in the Mazatzal Wilderness Area.
General location: Twenty-five miles southeast of Payson.
Maps: Chalk Mountain 7.5-minute, Table Mountain 7.5-minute, Cypress Butte

7.5-minute, Wet Bottom Mesa 7.5-minute, North Peak 7.5-minute USGS quads; USFS Mazatzal map.

Difficulty: Difficult (rough, faint trails).

Length: About 41 miles.

Elevation: 2,100 to 6,700 feet.

Special attractions: Varied life zones, from Sonoran desert to Transition pine forest; varied terrain, from desert flats to rocky escarpments and deep canyons.

Water availability: See description.

Best season: Spring and fall.

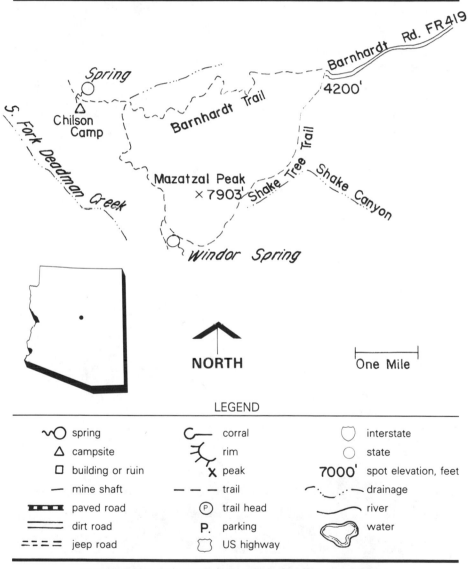

BARNHARDT-SHAKE TREE HIKE 36

The old sheep bridge spanning the Verde River was used for many years to move sheep from the desert lowlands to the highcountry. Stewart Aitchison

For more information: Payson Ranger District, P.O. Box 100, Payson, AZ 85541; (602) 474-2269.
Permit: None.

These trails are accessible from the Sheep Bridge Trailhead on the Verde River, one of the more remote trailheads in central Arizona. It can be approached two ways. From Carefree, north of Phoenix, take the Cave Creek Road (Forest Road 24) north approximately 30 miles to the Tangle Creek Road (Forest Road 269). Turn east (right) and drive about 10 miles to the Sheep Bridge Trailhead at the end of the road. This route is normally passable except during or after a major winter storm.

You can also reach the Tangle Creek Road via the Bloody Basin Road, by exiting I-17 about 2 miles south of Cordes Junction (80 miles north of Phoenix), and going east about 30 miles (during which the road becomes Forest Road 269 at the National Forest boundary). This road may be impassable after heavy rain or snow, especially at the Agua Fria River crossing about 5 miles from the freeway.

Despite the long drive, Sheep Bridge is a popular spot. The old footbridge was built by sheepherders to get their animals across the Verde for the long drive north to the highcountry west of Payson. Each year the sheep were moved from their low winter pastures to higher summer pastures and back. Today, historic Sheep Bridge is unsafe and has been closed by the Forest Service. Until it is replaced, hikers will have to ford the river, usually an easy and safe maneuver but dangerous during times of high runoff.

The loop trip described here samples some of the incredible variety of the Mazatzal country. Once across the river at the east end of Sheep Bridge, take the signed Willow Spring Trail east through the Sonoran desert foothills. The trail winds through stands of sahuaro and cholla cactus and ascends gradually

The highest point in the Mazatzal Wilderness is Mazatzal Peak at 7,888 feet. The mountain is composed of quartzite, a metamorphosed sandstone, formed nearly 2 billion years ago. Bruce Grubbs

the first several miles. About 3 miles from Sheep Bridge, it passes close to Horse Creek, easily identified by its tall cottonwood trees, where there is seasonal water. Three miles farther, the trail begins to climb steeply up to Willow Spring Basin (Willow Spring should be reliable) and from there even more steeply to Mountain Spring. Along the way, hikers pass from the saguaro-dominated Sonoran desert to high desert grassland and then to pinyon-juniper woodland. Mountain Spring should be reliable. Both Willow Spring and Mountain Spring are fine campsites.

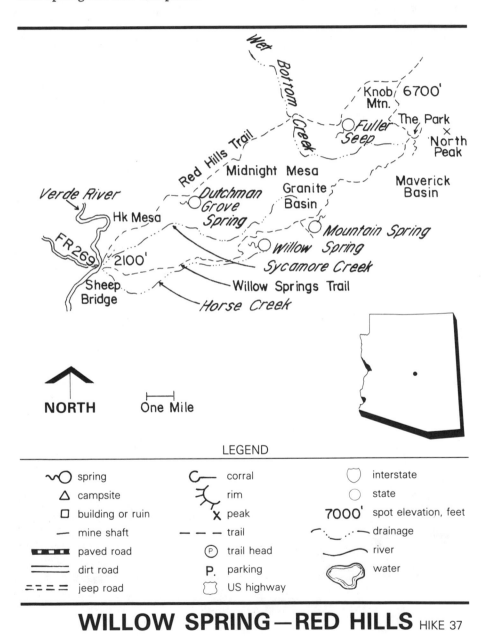

WILLOW SPRING—RED HILLS HIKE 37

The trail climbs over a ridge above Mountain Spring, then works its way northeast along a ridge system toward Midnight Mesa, passing Lost Spring (not shown on the USGS map). It swings around the east end of Midnight Mesa, offering fine views of the rugged Maverick Basin area, then descends through stands of Arizona cypress to cross an arm of Wet Bottom Creek. There will be water here in wet years. In dry years, however, you may have to carry water for camp or else continue north on the Red Hills cutoff trail and camp at the Wet Bottom Creek crossing, which should have water in winter and spring. As its name implies, this trail is a shortcut to the Red Hills Trail, and it leaves the Willow Spring Trail just northeast of Midnight Mesa.

The Willow Spring Trail continues northeast from the creek crossing, climbing steeply (again) onto a pine-covered ridge above Maverick Basin, the head of Deadman Creek. It passes through a saddle before contouring north to end at the Divide Trail. There is an unsigned remnant of an old trail shown on the map at the saddle. This is the old Divide Trail. The new Divide Trail junction is just off the edge of the Cypress Butte quad, on the North Peak map.

Now follow the Divide Trail north to The Park, the head of Wetbottom Creek, which drains most of the northwestern Mazatzals. Here is the junction with the North Peak Trail, a steep but scenic route down the north side of North Peak. The Divide Trail now swings west around a canyon head (where there is seasonal water) and then north over the gentle slopes of Knob Mountain, the high point of the trip at about 6,700 feet. The trail shown on the Cypress Butte quad going west across Knob Mountain is virtually nonexistent, although the route can be followed cross-country.

Continue north on the Divide Trail a mile to the signed junction with the Red Hills Trail, shown on the wilderness map but not the USGS map. Although it is shorter to take the cross-country route across Knob Mountain, this first part of the Red Hills Trail makes going out of your way worthwhile. The Red Hills trail descends the ridge as shown on the topo for a short distance but then turns abruptly west (don't take the old trail down the ridge!) and descends into the head of Boardinghouse Canyon. This area is heavily forested with ponderosa pines and offers a number of nice campsites with water during the cool season.

After about a mile, the trail climbs up another drainage to the northwest side of Knob Mountain and passes the junction with the Wet Bottom Trail. It turns south and drops steeply into the Fuller Seep basin. The seep seems to be reliable and there is good camping in this scenic basin. From here the trail climbs over a ridge, past the junction with the Red Hills cutoff trail, and then works its way down to Wet Bottom Creek. This section of the trail is fainter and may require use of the wilderness map in conjunction with the Cypress Butte quad.

Across the creek, the trail climbs steeply to the top of a cypress-covered ridge, then wanders in a half-circle to the north across the mesa top. The trail is faint and it will be necessary to carefully watch for cairns. You do NOT want to lose the trail. Cross-country hiking in this area is rough and slow.

About 2.5 miles from Wet Bottom Creek, the trail reaches a saddle and turns abruptly west, descending into a drainage (one of the many arms of Wet Bottom Creek). There is camping and seasonal water where the trail crosses the drainage and climbs out to the south. Once on top of the mesa, it swings around to the northwest, then descends to a saddle and drops steeply to an obvious mine in the canyon to the southwest. At the mouth of the canyon, you have abruptly re-entered the land of giant saguaros. The trail continues about 2 miles south over rolling hills, paralleling a drainage, past the turnoff to Dutchman Grave Spring (which should be reliable). The trail turns west, crosses the drainage, and climbs over a low ridge. On the far side it swings onto HK Mesa and follows the top of the mesa southwest, paralleling the lush drainage of Sycamore Creek, a permanent source of water. At the end of the mesa, Sheep Bridge will be in sight, only a mile away.—*Bruce Grubbs* □

HIKE 38   *MOUNT BALDY*

General description: A round-trip day hike or longer into the Mount Baldy Wilderness Area.
General location: Fifteen miles southwest of Springerville.
Maps: Mt. Ord 7.5-minute USGS quad; USFS Mount Baldy Wilderness map.
Difficulty: Moderate.
Length: Seven miles one way.
Elevation: 9,200 to 11,400 feet.
Special attractions: Views of the White Mountains, alpine environment.
Water availability: West Fork of the Little Colorado River, occasional small side streams.
Best season: Summer through fall.

When hiking along the summit ridge to Mount Baldy, please stay on the trail. The fragile alpine plants are easily damaged by trampling. As you approach the summit, the spruce and alpine-fir trees become stunted and twisted. This forest community is called krummholz, from the German word meaning "crooked wood," and is a common feature just below timberline on a mountain. Bruce Grubbs

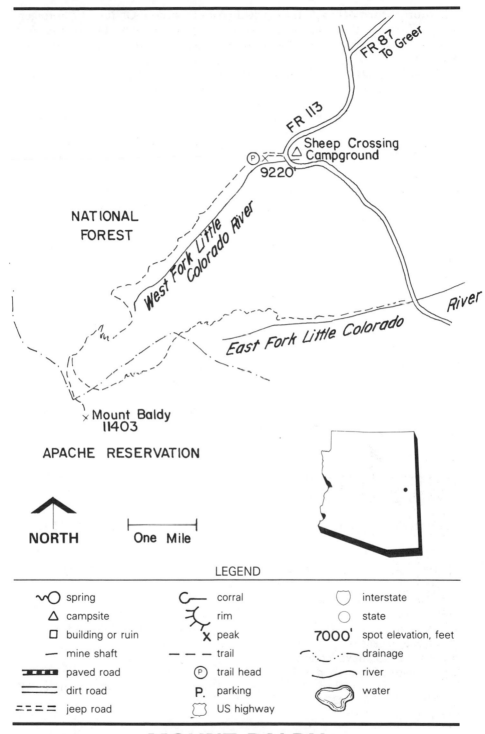

FR 87 To Greer

FR 113

Sheep Crossing
Campground

9220'

NATIONAL
FOREST

West Fork Little Colorado River

East Fork Little Colorado River

× Mount Baldy
11403

APACHE RESERVATION

NORTH

One Mile

LEGEND

∿O	spring	C	corral	◠	interstate	
△	campsite	⋎	rim	◯	state	
▫	building or ruin	X	peak	7000'	spot elevation, feet	
—	mine shaft	– – –	trail	⌇	drainage	
▰▰▰	paved road	Ⓟ	trail head	⌇	river	
===	dirt road	P.	parking	▨	water	
= = = =	jeep road	⬠	US highway			

MOUNT BALDY HIKE 38

For more information: Springerville Ranger District, P.O. Box 640, Springerville, AZ 86938; (602) 333-4372; White Mountain Apache Enterprise, Fort Apache Indian Reservation, P.O. Box 218, Whiteriver, AZ 85941; (602) 338-4385.

Permit: None for Forest Service land, but the summit is closed (see description below).

Begin this popular hike by taking Forest Road 87 out of Greer about 6 miles to its junction with Forest Road 113. Turn left and drive about 2 miles to the Sheep Crossing Campground. The signed trailhead is located here.

The trail begins along the right bank of the West Fork of the Little Colorado River and climbs through wonderful blue spruce forest and alpine meadows where in summer aster, fleabane, penstemon, cinquefoil, and iris bloom. There is evidence of past glacial activity—glacial erratics, large boulders deposited by ice, lie along the canyon floor.

West Fork contains brook, rainbow, and cutthroat trout but the trail is only close to the stream near the trailhead. About 3 miles from the trailhead, the trail crosses a tributary to West Fork. In another 2 miles it reaches the ridge leading to Baldy Peak. Then a mile from the summit, the East Fork Trail joins your route.

As you near the summit, you are treated to spectacular vistas of the White Mountain region including recent clear-cutting scars on the Apache Reservation and their new downhill ski development.

Within .3 mile from the top, you reach the Apache Reservation boundary—the Apaches have closed the last section of trail to the top, so this boundary must serve as the turnaround point for most hikers. You might be able to secure a permit by writing to the Apaches at the address above. It's not worth "sneaking" to the summit, however, since several hikers have been caught and their packs confiscated.—*Stewart Aitchison* □

HIKE 39 *ESCUDILLA MOUNTAIN*

General description: A round-trip day hike into the Escudilla Wilderness Area.

General location: Eight miles north of Alpine.

Maps: Alpine 15-minute USGS quad; Apache National Forest map.

Difficulty: Moderate.

Length: Two miles one way.

Elevation: 9,480 to 10,876 feet.

Special attractions: One of the places that inspired Aldo Leopold to write about wilderness.

Water availability: None.

Best season: Summer and fall.

For more information: Alpine Ranger District, P.O. Box 469, Alpine, AZ 85920; (602) 339-4384.

Permit: None.

This hike features two trailheads, both accessible by driving about 6 miles

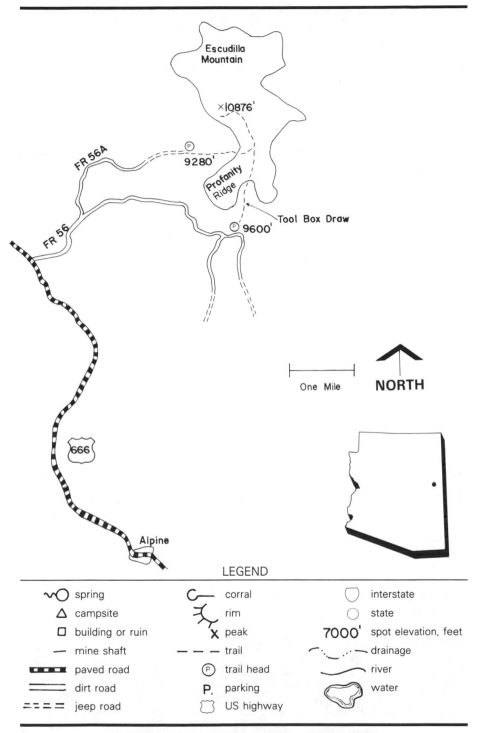

Escudilla
Mountain

×10876'

FR 56A

P
9280'

Profanity
Ridge

Tool Box Draw

FR 56

P
9600'

|—————|
One Mile

NORTH

666

Alpine

LEGEND

∿○	spring	ᑕ—	corral	◯	interstate
△	campsite	⅄	rim	◯	state
▢	building or ruin	**X**	peak	**7000'**	spot elevation, feet
—	mine shaft	– – –	trail	⌒⋯⋯⋯⋯	drainage
▰▰▰▰	paved road	Ⓟ	trail head	⌒⌒	river
═══	dirt road	**P.**	parking	⬭	water
═ ═ ═	jeep road	⬠	US highway		

ESCUDILLA MOUNTAIN HIKE 39

north of Alpine on U.S. 666. Turn right onto Forest Road 56. In about 1.5 miles you come to a fork. The left fork, FR 56A, goes a couple of miles and then ends at the Government Trail; the right fork winds a couple of miles along the southern base of the mountain and just before turning away to the south, the Escudilla National Recreation Trail begins. The trailheads may not be signed.

Both trails take you through stands of virgin pine, fir, and spruce to the viewpoint at the lookout, your turnaround point. The Escudilla National Recreation Trail is slightly less steep.

Escudilla Mountain received a little notoriety in conservationist Aldo Leopold's classic work *A Sand County Almanac* as the location where one of the last grizzly bears in Arizona was killed. Today black bear, wild turkeys, and deer still roam the mountain.—*Stewart Aitchison*

HIKE 40 *BEAR WALLOW*

General description: A long, round-trip day hike into the Bear Wallow Wilderness Area.
General location: Seven miles southwest of Hannagan Meadow.
Maps: Hannagan Meadow 15-minute USGS quad; Apache National Forest map.
Difficulty: Moderate.
Length: Up to 7.6 miles one way.
Elevation: 6,700 to 8,700 feet.
Special attractions: Running stream in dense coniferous forest.

Mule deer are common residents of Arizona highcountry. Their large ears always tuned for danger. Deer in the low desert areas tend to be Sonoran white-tailed deer. Stewart Aitchison

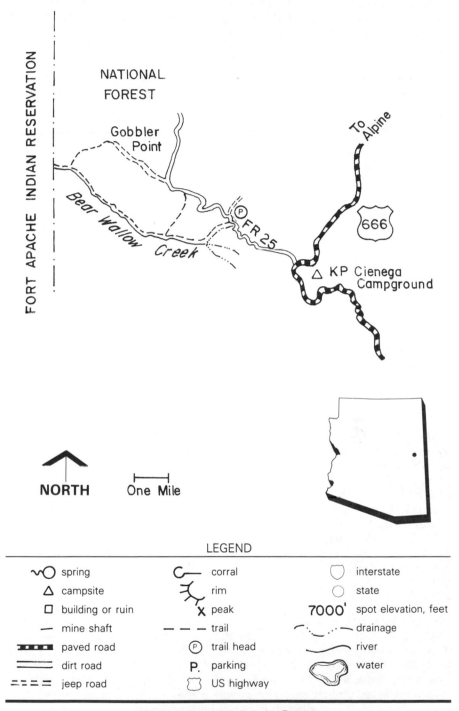

NATIONAL FOREST

FORT APACHE INDIAN RESERVATION

Gobbler Point

Bear Wallow Creek

To Alpine

666

P FR 25

△ KP Cienega Campground

NORTH

One Mile

LEGEND

∿O	spring	C—	corral	◯	interstate
△	campsite	⅄	rim	◯	state
▢	building or ruin	X	peak	7000'	spot elevation, feet
—	mine shaft	– – –	trail	⌒⋅⋅⋅⌒	drainage
▬▬▬	paved road	P	trail head	⌒	river
═══	dirt road	P.	parking	⬡	water
≡≡≡	jeep road	⬡	US highway		

BEAR WALLOW HIKE 40

Water availability: Stream is permanent.
Best season: Summer and fall.
For more information: Alpine Ranger District, P.O. Box 469, Alpine, AZ 85920; (602) 339-4384.
Permit: None.

From Hannagan Meadow, drive about 6 miles south on U.S. 666. Turn right onto Forest Road 25; drive about 4 miles to the junction with Forest Road 25B and park. Your trail, Forest Trail 63, starts here and heads left (south) as a logging road. The foot trail begins after about 80 yards.

This hike follows the length of the drainage. At mile 2.6, this trail intersects with the Reno Trail (Forest Trail 62), and at mile 7.1 it intersects the Gobbler Point Trail (Forest Trail 59). The Bear Wallow Trail ends abruptly at the San Carlos Indian Reservation boundary, which is marked by a fence and serves as your turnaround point.

The dominant vegetation here is the riparian habitat along the creek with mature ponderosa pine and Gambel oak on the south-facing slopes. The north-facing slopes have mostly spruce and firs. Currently fishing is not allowed in the creek.

Pete Slaughter in 1884 drove cattle into this valley and saw the numerous bear wallows along the creek where the bears came to ward off pesky flies. Black bears still roam the valley, as do elk, mulk deer, and mountain lion.— *Apache National Forest* □

HIKE 41 *BEAR VALLEY*

General description: A round-trip backpack into the Blue Range Primitive Area.
General location: Ten miles southeast of Hannagan Meadow.
Maps: Dutch Blue Creek 7.5 minute USGS quad; Alma Mesa 7.5 minute USGS quad; Blue 15-minute USGS quad; Apache National Forest map.
Difficulty: Difficult, trail obscured by cattle paths.
Length: About 10 miles one way.
Elevation: 4,800 to 6,900 feet.
Special attractions: Great views of the southern Blue Range and beyond.
Water availability: Landron Springs and Little Blue Spring are reliable; Auger Tank is questionable.
Best season: Spring through fall, although summer can be quite hot.
For more information: Clifton Ranger District, Box 698, Clifton, AZ; (602) 865-2432.
Permit: None.

The Bear Valley trail is a scenic route with an abundance of spectacular views of the southern portion of the Blue Range and beyond. To reach the trailhead, drive 4 miles east of Alpine on U.S. 180 and turn south onto Forest Road 281 (also called the Blue River Road). Drive to its southern dead end at a cabin, barn, and corral known as the Smith Place. The last 2 miles of road include several river crossings which may be impassable during high water. Remember that discretion is the better part of valor, especially in a remote area such as this

The signed Blue River Trail (Forest Trail 101) begins at the Smith Place and follows the river downstream. After hiking about 3 miles, you intersect the Bear Valley Trail (Forest Trail 55) at the mouth of the Landron Springs drainage. A trail sign is maintained on a large cottonwood there.

The Bear Valley Trail starts out on the north side of the Landron Springs drainage and passes several small waterfalls. The trail crosses the drainage twice before arriving at Landron Springs, a powerful and constant spring emerging near the base of a large walnut tree. The spring creates a virtual oasis in an otherwise dry setting.

The trail crosses an open area above the springs, contours along conglomerate ash tuff bedrock, and then descends to an old corral in Sycamore Canyon. The trail crosses the canyon going beneath a lone mature sycamore tree, then climbs a gentle slope through mesquite and bedrock to a saddle. The trail crosses the saddle to the east and switchbacks up the ridge, eventually contouring to the north through some rock bluffs. There are exceptional views along this portion of trail.

The route continues northward over a saddle and then descends to cross Auger Canyon at Auger Tank. Usually there is water here, but you may need to rattle the pipe to get it flowing. Cross directly over the dam and then the low point of Auger Mesa. The trail continues across the south fork of Auger Creek and then heads up the north slope of Government Mesa. The ascent is steep and rocky. The top of the mesa has juniper, cactus, and bear grass.

The trail heads east along the ridgeline of Government Mesa and then makes another ascent to Juniper Flats. Finally it follows a drainage down into Bear Valley, where it meets the Little Blue Trail (Forest Trail 41).

Follow the Little Blue Trail right, past an old cabin to a corral, the turnaround point of the hike. There is often water in the drainage below the cabin.

Deep in the Blue Range Primitive Area, long and difficult access routes have kept out all but the most dedicated hikers. For those of you looking for solitude, this is the place.
Bruce Grubbs

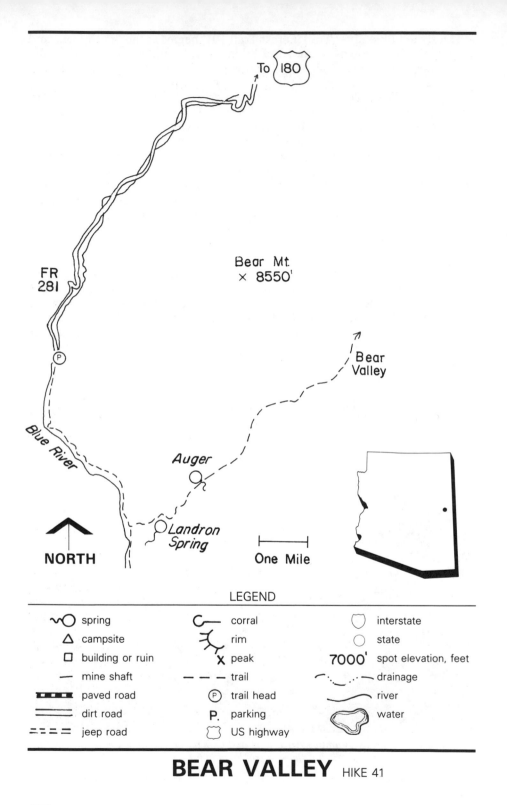

To 180

Bear Mt.
× 8550'

FR
281

Bear
Valley

Blue River

Auger

Landron
Spring

NORTH

One Mile

LEGEND

spring		corral		interstate	
campsite		rim		state	
building or ruin		peak		7000' spot elevation, feet	
mine shaft		trail		drainage	
paved road		trail head		river	
dirt road		parking		water	
jeep road		US highway			

BEAR VALLEY HIKE 41

If not, there is dependable water .75 mile farther down-trail in Little Blue Canyon.

Bear Valley was farmed at the turn of the century, and there are remains of an old wagon and a few outbuildings scattered throughout the valley.—*Apache National Forest* □

HIKE 42 *BEAR MOUNTAIN*

General description: A two-day loop hike in the Blue Range Primitive Area.
General location: Twenty-five miles south of Alpine.
Maps: Blue 15-minute USGS quad; Apache-Sitgreaves National Forest map.
Difficulty: Moderate.
Length: About 15 miles.
Elevation: 5,700 to 7,800 feet.
Special attractions: High, cool pine-and-fir forest.
Water availability: Lower Lanphier Canyon, Cashier Spring, Maple Spring.
Best season: May through November.
For more information: Alpine Ranger District, P.O. Box 469, Alpine, AZ 85920; (602) 339-4384.
Permit: None.

From Alpine, drive east a couple of miles on U.S. 180 and turn south on Forest Road 281. Stay on this road past the junction with Forest Road 232 to the Forest Service's Blue Administrative Site. The Largo Creek-Lanphier Creek Trailhead is signed.

Most of the Blue Range Primitive Area is seldom visited by hikers and offers a taste of backpacking far from the crowds that haunt other areas. The Blue fully deserves but has never attained congressional protection as a Wilderness Area.

Many of the trails in the Blue Range are faint because of disuse and require some care to follow. The topographic map is a must! From the trailhead, take Forest Trail 51 across the Blue River (please respect the right of way through private land) and on up Lanphier Canyon. After about a mile, Trail 51, your return route, branches off to the right—stay on the Lanphier Trail 52. There is normally running water in the first several miles of Lanphier Creek as the trail ascends through fine stands of ponderosa pine. About 3 miles from the Blue River, the trail leaves the creek for more than a mile. There is limited camping where the trail meets the creek again.

Cashier Spring is probably reliable and is the last likely water source until the trail descends to Maple Spring in Largo Creek on the return. After wet winters, most of these drainages will be running with water, but in dry autumns the water situation can be more serious.

Above Cashier Spring the trail ends at a signed junction. Take Forest Trail 55 right to Campbell Flat. This section of trail wanders through open stands of ponderosa pine and offers numerous campsites, all without water. At Campbell Flat the trail reaches the Mogollon Rim. Turn west at the signed junction onto Forest Trail 54.

This trail wanders west along the hilly rim for several miles, passing through

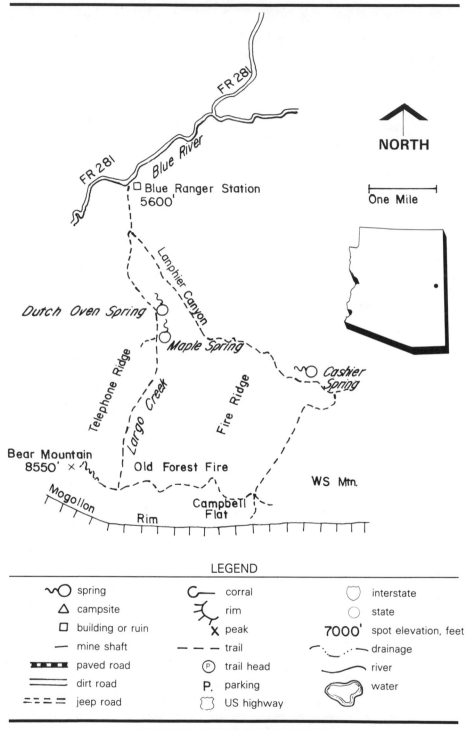

FR 281

FR 281

Blue River

NORTH

One Mile

☐ Blue Ranger Station
5600'

Lanphier Canyon

Dutch Oven Spring

Maple Spring

Cashier Spring

Telephone Ridge

Largo Creek

Fire Ridge

Bear Mountain
8550' ×

Old Forest Fire

WS Mtn.

Mogollon

Rim

Campbell
Flat

LEGEND

ᔕO	spring	C⟋	corral	◯	interstate
△	campsite	⟋	rim	◯	state
☐	building or ruin	X	peak	7000'	spot elevation, feet
—	mine shaft	– – –	trail	⟋⋯⟍	drainage
▨▨	paved road	Ⓟ	trail head	⟋⟍	river
══	dirt road	P.	parking	◌	water
= = =	jeep road	⬡	US highway		

BEAR MOUNTAIN HIKE 42

a large burn and eventually reaching a junction with the signed Largo Canyon Trail (Forest Trail 51) at a saddle just below Bear Mountain. It is an easy side trip up to Bear Mountain Lookout, which is manned during the summer fire season.

The Largo Canyon Trail descends into the upper reaches of the creek, where there is seasonal water and several campsites. The signed Telephone Ridge Trail (Forest Trail 42) joins your route, and there should be water at Maple Spring or Dutch Oven Spring and limited camping in this stretch of the canyon. The trail follows Largo Creek to within a mile of the Blue River, then climbs over the ridge to the northeast and descends to the Lanphier Trail. Turn left and retrace your earlier steps about a mile to the trailhead.—*Bruce Grubbs* □

HIKE 43 *ALGONQUIN*

General description: A long, round-trip day hike or leisurely two-day round-trip hike in the Castle Creek Wilderness Area.
General location: Four miles south of Crown King.
Maps: Crown King 7.5-minute USGS quad; Prescott National Forest map.
Difficulty: Moderate.
Length: About 4 miles one way.
Elevation: 6,850 to 4,600 feet.
Special attractions: Rugged canyons, historic mining areas.
Water availability: Seasonal in Poland Creek and Horsethief Creek.
Best season: April through November.
For more information: Bradshaw Ranger District, RFD 7, Box 3451, Prescott, AZ 86301; (602) 445-7253.
Permit: None.

From Interstate 17, take the Bumblebee Exit north of Black Canyon City and drive approximately 30 miles on Forest Road 259 to the old mining town of Crown King (now a summer-home community). Continue south on FR 259 for .5 mile and go south (left) on Forest Road 52 another 2.5 miles to the signed trailhead on the east (left) for Trail 225. This trail is not shown on the topo map.

The trail starts in a forested flat on the broad ridgetop, then traverses north along the east slopes of Juniper Ridge. About a mile from the trailhead, it drops onto a ridge and then plunges steeply into Horsethief Canyon through rocky and brushy terrain. At the canyon bottom, your trail joins the signed Horsethief Trail. Turn left (north) on this trail and follow it .25 mile to the site of the old Algonquin Mine, the original reason for these trails and most others in the Bradshaw Mountains. Only a few twisted pieces of rail are visible now near the collapsed mouth of the mine, but the ruins and outlines of several cabins are nearby.

The trail continues north (along a section which was improved as a wagon road when the mine was active) to the Crown King Road. The Horsethief Trail climbs south along scenic Horsethief Canyon to the Horsethief Basin Recreation Area.

There are a number of other trails in this area suitable for dayhikes and overnight backpack trips.—*Bruce Grubbs* □

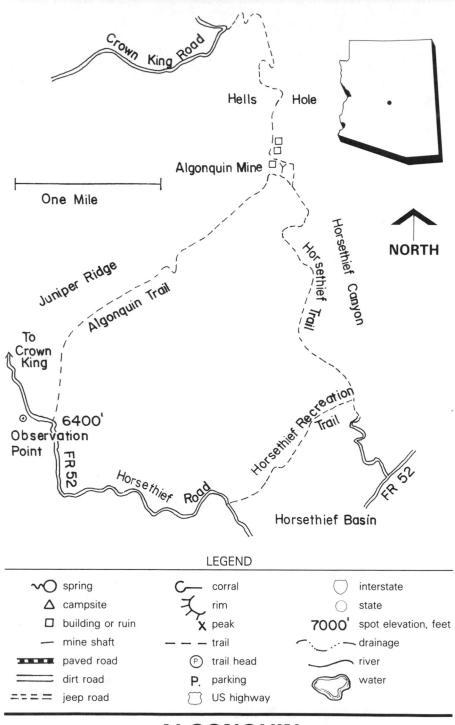

One Mile

Crown King Road

Hells Hole

Algonquin Mine

Juniper Ridge

Algonquin Trail

Horsethief Trail

Horsethief Canyon

NORTH

To Crown King

6400'
Observation Point

FR 52

Horsethief Recreation Trail

Horsethief Road

FR 52

Horsethief Basin

LEGEND

᠊ᴑ	spring	C	corral	◯	interstate	
△	campsite	⅄	rim	◯	state	
□	building or ruin	X	peak	7000'	spot elevation, feet	
—	mine shaft	– – –	trail	⌒·⌒··⌒	drainage	
▬▬▬	paved road	Ⓟ	trail head		river	
═══	dirt road	P.	parking		water	
≡≡≡	jeep road	⬡	US highway			

ALGONQUIN HIKE 43

HIKE 44 *BLACK CANYON*

General description: A round-trip day hike in cool pine forest.
General location: South end of Mingus Mountain.
Maps: Cottonwood 7.5-minute USGS quad; Prescott National Forest map.
Difficulty: Moderate.
Length: About 6 miles one way.
Elevation: 6,600 to 4,200 feet.

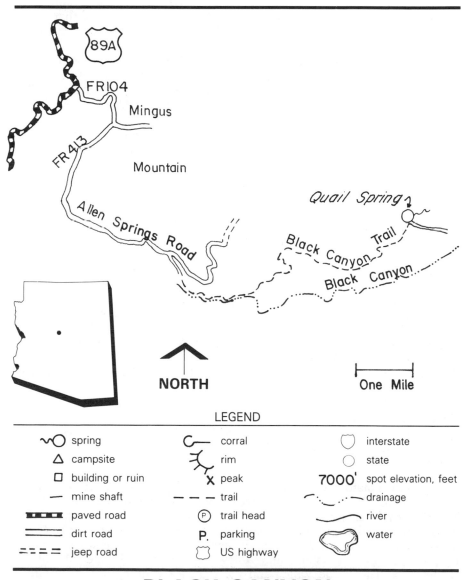

NORTH

One Mile

LEGEND

∿O	spring	C⌒	corral	⬭	interstate
△	campsite		rim	◯	state
▢	building or ruin	X	peak	**7000'**	spot elevation, feet
—	mine shaft	– – –	trail	⌒‥⌒	drainage
▪▪▪▪	paved road	Ⓟ	trail head		river
══	dirt road	P.	parking	⬭	water
=：=	jeep road	⌂	US highway		

BLACK CANYON HIKE 44

Water availability: Seasonal in Black Canyon.
Special attractions: Cool pine forest, live stream, waterfalls.
Best season: May through November.
For more information: Verde Ranger District, HC 62, Box 1100, Camp Verde, AZ 86322: (602) 567-4121.
Permit: None.
Wilderness status: None.

Take U.S. 89A to the top of Mingus Mountain, east of Prescott, and turn south on Forest Road 104. After about 1.5 miles, turn west (right) on Forest Road 413, the Allen Springs Road. This road is passable to most vehicles as far as the Black Canyon Trail but becomes much rougher beyond that point. A little more than 5 miles from Forest Road 104, watch for the signed trailhead for Black Canyon Trail 114.

The trail follows Gaddes Canyon into the gentle forested valley at the head of Black Canyon. About 2 miles from the road it veers north out of the creekbed and drops down the slopes north of the canyon, ending after about 4 miles at Quail Springs and the end of Forest Road 359 (accessible from the Verde Valley). This is your turnaround point.

It is possible to descend Black Canyon below the point where the trail leaves the canyon. This is a very rugged but interesting scramble down ledges and waterfalls. You can then take the trail back to your car.—*Bruce Grubbs* □

HIKE 45 *WOODCHUTE*

General description: A round-trip day hike in the Woodchute Wilderness Area.
General location: North end of Mingus Mountain.
Maps: Mingus Mountain 15-minute USGS quad; Prescott National Forest map.
Difficulty: Easy.
Length: Five miles one way to north rim of Woodchute Mountain.
Elevation: 7,000 to 7,700 feet.
Special attractions: Easy hiking, fine views of the Verde Valley, Chino Valley, and Sycamore Canyon.
Water availability: None.
Best season: May through October.
For more information: Verde Ranger District, HC 62, Box 1100, Camp Verde, AZ 86322; (602) 567-4121.
Permit: None.

Park at the Potato Patch Campground just off U.S. 89A, east of the Mingus Mountain pass. Follow a jeep trail west, then north out of the campground. Trail 102 leaves the jeep road just north of Powerline Tank and works its way north about 4 miles through mixed pinyon and ponderosa pine forest to the north rim of Woodchute Mountain. In several places, the trail ascends along ridges which offer views of Chino Valley and the remote Juniper Mountains to the west. The Verde Valley and the red rock country near Oak Creek Canyon are also visible.

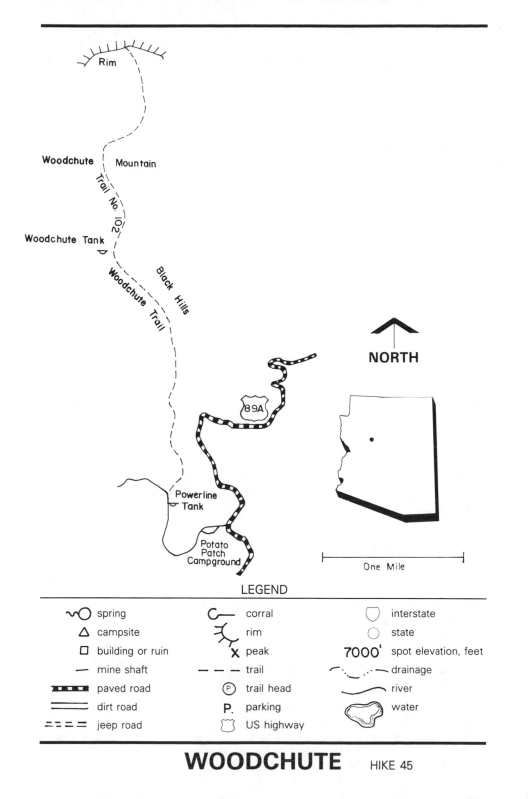

LEGEND

∿○	spring	⌐	corral	⬠	interstate
△	campsite		rim	◯	state
☐	building or ruin	X	peak	7000'	spot elevation, feet
—	mine shaft	– – –	trail		drainage
▬▬▬	paved road	Ⓟ	trail head		river
══	dirt road	P.	parking		water
= = =	jeep road	⬡	US highway		

WOODCHUTE   HIKE 45

The north rim of Woodchute Mountain offers expansive views of the Sycamore Canyon Wilderness Area and the red rock country west of Sedona, as well as of the San Francisco Peaks and the Mogollon Rim. The trail continues down the steep slope to end at Forest Road 318A just off the Perkinsville-Jerome road. Return the way you came.—*Bruce Grubbs* □

HIKE 46   *POACHIE RANGE*

General description: Exploratory hikes in rugged granitic and lava mountains covered with unusual mixture of plant species.
General location: Fifty miles northwest of Wickenburg.
Maps: Arrastra Mountain 7.5-minute, Arrastra Mountain NE 7.5-minute, Arrastra Mountain SE 7.5-minute, Palmerita Ranch 7.5-minute, Artillery Peak 15-minute USGS quads.
Difficulty: Easy to difficult (cross-country).
Permit: None.
Wilderness status: BLM Wilderness Study Area.

This BLM Wilderness Study Area does not have any designated trails; however, cross-country travel is fairly easy and adds to hikers' sense of discovery.

The bite of the giant desert centipede is painful but otherwise is not a serious injury. The tip of each of the centipede's forty-two legs is equipped with a sharp claw which may make pin-point punctures, but a double pair of jaws under the head do the actual biting. Unless you make a habit of putting your bare hand under rocks or into crevices, you are unlikely to be bitten. Bruce Grubbs

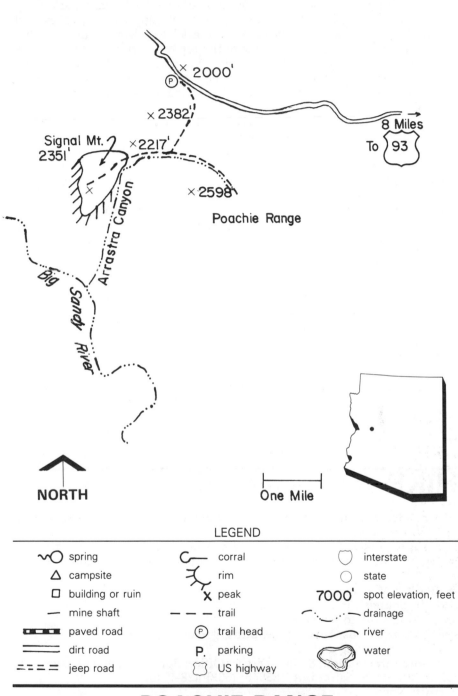

× 2000'

P

× 2382'

Signal Mt.
2351'

× 2217'

Arrastra Canyon

× 2598

Poachie Range

Big Sandy River

8 Miles

To 93

NORTH

One Mile

POACHIE RANGE HIKE 46

One approach is to turn off of Arizona 93 about 50 miles northwest of Wickenburg (mile post 132). Drive south about 9 miles and then turn left onto an unsigned but well-graded road. Drive another 3.2 miles and park along the edge of the road. From here hike due south, crossing several washes, and then pick a path of least resistance over the black lava ridges and mesas facing you. You will encounter an old fence at the top of the ridge. Once over the fence, there are many options for hiking. One is to go to the top of Signal Mountain to the southwest; another is to follow one of the several main washes upstream to narrow granite gorges similiar to the inner gorge of the Grand Canyon.

The desert vegetation consists of such typical Sonoran species as catclaw acacia, ocotillo, saguaro, barrel cactus, beavertail cactus, desert willow, creosote bush, palo verde, brittlebush, and Bigelow nolina. Mixed in with these are Mohave Desert species of yucca, false palo verde, sugar sumac, and desert trumpet. Mormon tea, snakeweed, and juniper are also present, species more typical of the Great Basin Desert.

Several species of cholla are common, including the fuzzy-looking but painful teddy bear jumping cholla. A slight brush against this plant causes a joint or section of stem to break off and stick to you. On top of Signal Mountain are clumps of Christmas cholla, often with bright red fruit.

Common residents of this area include Yuma antelope squirrels which look like chipmunks, mule deer, cactus mice, white-throated wood rats, pocket mice, kangaroo rats, black-tailed jackrabbits, and desert cottontails. Feral burros and a few cows also wander the area. On a sunny November day hikers can expect to see the following birds, among others: rock wrens, canyon wrens, cactus wrens, red-tailed hawks, golden eagles, curve-billed thrashers, Gambel's quail, northern flickers, Gila woodpeckers, phainopepla, black-tailed gnat-catchers, and dark-eyed juncoes.

Unfortunately, hikers are also more likely to see pieces of desert tortoise shell than they are to see live tortoises. The desert tortoise population has suffered greatly from livestock overgrazing.—*Stewart Aitchison* □

HIKE 47 *SAFFORD-MORENCI*

General description: A point-to-point, two-day or longer backpack trip into an historical area.
General location: Twelve miles northeast of Safford.
Maps: Safford 15-minute, Bryce Mtn. 15-minute, Clifton 15-minute USGS quads.
Difficulty: Moderate.
Length: Fourteen miles one way.
Elevation: 3,700 to 6,000 feet.
Special attractions: Scenic pass, birds, geology, history.
Best season: Spring and fall.
For more information: Safford District Office, Bureau of Land Managment, 425 E. 4th Street, Safford, AZ 85546; (602) 428-4040.
Permit: None.
Wilderness status: BLM Wilderness Study Area.

To locate the trailhead, drive northeast out of Safford on the San Juan Road. About 8 miles down this road, take the left fork heading for Walnut Springs and West Ranch. The trailhead is signed. It is 14 miles to the end of the trail at the East Trailhead.

By arranging a car shuttle, however, you can avoid having to re-hike the fourteen miles. To do this, drive west out of Morenci on the Eagle Creek Road about 5 miles and leave a car parked at the East Trailhead.

During wet weather, both roads may be impassable to two-wheel-drive vehicles.

From the Safford-Morenci trailhead, this well-established trail winds through rugged and beautiful canyons with elevations ranging from 3,700 feet to more than 6,000 feet. You will encounter a variety of vegetation types and species, ranging from mesquite and creosote bush at the West Ranch trailhead; to riparian plants like cottonwood, willow, and sycamore along Bonita Creek; to pinyon-juniper and oak in Smith Canyon.

Geological types vary among rhyolite, andesite, and basalt, which together produce majestic rock outcrops and multi-colored formations.

The area provides habitat for mule deer, mountain lion, javelina, rabbit, dove, quail, and a variety of other Sonoran desert species. Bonita Creek is the best area along this hike to see a wide variety of birds, including hawks and eagles.

Cultural features range from prehistoric Indian cliff dwellings in Bonita Creek to remnants of early-day homesteads.

With the advent of the the automobile in the early 1900s, the trail ceased to be used. Recently, however, the Youth Conservation Corps reconditioned the trail for hikers and horseback riders. Please sign the register at the trailhead.

Bring an ample supply of water for this hike, since streams and springs are scarce. Also purify any water found along the trail before drinking it.

Pioneer farmers and ranchers in the Gila Valley and Bonita Creek area gouged out the Safford-Morenci Trail about 1874. They needed a shorter route to Morenci, Metcalf, and Clifton, where booming mines offered a market for their produce and meat. Also, as the mines developed and the need for wood to burn in the smelters increased, Mexican wood haulers and their pack trains of mules and burros used the trail to haul wood for sale to the copper companies.

Horse rancher Albert Bellmeyer and his foreman rode up this trail from the Morenci side on October 25, 1892. Six years earlier, Geronimo had surrendered, ending for all practical purposes the threat to settlers from hostile Indians. However, renegades had left the San Carlos Reservation for forays as far south as Mexico, 125 miles away. Reports that Indians had been seen on Turtle Mountain prompted Bellmeyer to check on his horse herd grazing on the mountain.

What exactly occurred or the sequence of events is conjecture. But evidence at the scene indicates that Bellmeyer and his foreman, a man named Gordonier, were ambushed and had no opportunity to defend themselves. Bellmeyer was shot twice and apparently died instantly, falling from his horse at the notch or 'saddle' in the mountain. The two quick shots apparently gave Gordonier a split-secong warning, and he wheeled his horse and spurred the frightened animal down the Bonita Creek side of the mountain. But 100 yards down the trail, Gordonier was hit and fell from his horse. The wound was not fatal and the Indians crushed his head with rocks.

When a man named Ben Parks found the bodies and alerted authorities in Morenci, a posse was dispatched to search for the murderers. Other volunteers tied the bodies on mules and took them to Morenci for burial. Before they

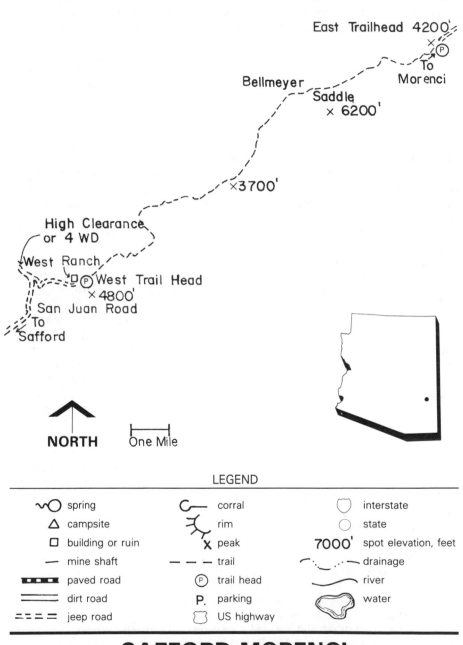

East Trailhead 4200'

×
Ⓟ

To
Morenci

Bellmeyer

Saddle
× 6200'

×3700'

High Clearance
or 4 WD

West Ranch

Ⓟ West Trail Head
× 4800'

San Juan Road

To
Safford

NORTH   One Mile

LEGEND

∿○	spring	C⟋	corral	⬡	interstate
△	campsite	⅄	rim	○	state
☐	building or ruin	X	peak	**7000'**	spot elevation, feet
—	mine shaft	– – –	trail	⌒‥⌒	drainage
▪▪▪▪	paved road	Ⓟ	trail head	⌒⌒	river
═══	dirt road	P.	parking	⬭	water
═ ═ ═	jeep road	⬯	US highway		

SAFFORD-MORENCI HIKE 47

left, they piled rocks beside the trail where each man had fallen. The point where the murders occurred was named Bellmeyer Saddle.

The guilty parties were never caught and their identities never known for sure. The infamous Apache Kid and two other renegades, Chato and Natchez, were suspected.

Some of the other people of note who lived near the trail included Toppy Johnson, whose real name was Presley Cantrell. Before coming to Arizona, he had served time in the Santa Fe prison for cattle rustling. Another group of local residents was the Fulchers, who were involved in the illegal horse-trading business. Mother Fulcher committed suicide on Bonita Creek where the trail crosses the creek. Two young cowboys named Putt Golding and Shorty Eaton loaded her remains onto a large mule and transported her via the trail to Morenci. These are just small chapters of the fascinating history associated with this trail.—*BLM, Safford District Office* □

The eerie howl of the coyote is an integral part of the wilderness. Considered a destructive varmint by many ranchers, the coyote nonetheless helps control rabbits, mice, and other rodents. It is also one of the few mammals that has increased its range over the last two centuries in spite of vigorous predator control programs. Stewart Aitchison

HIKE 48 *ARAVAIPA CANYON*

General description: A point-to-point or round-trip hike featuring easy walking and splashing through a creek into a colorful canyon amid Sonoran desert vegetation in the Aravaipa Canyon Wilderness Area.

General location: About 11 miles south and 10 miles east of Winkleman.

Maps: Brandenburg Mountain 7.5-minute, Booger Canyon 7.5-minute USGS quads.

Difficulty: Easy.

Length: 10.75 miles one way to traverse canyon.

Elevation: 2,600 to 3,100 feet.

Special attractions: Wading through a cool stream while hiking a desert canyon; more than three hundred species of vertebrates including native fish, desert bighorn, mountain lion, and peregrine falcon.

Best season: Spring, summer, or fall. Avoid periods of high water, particularly summertime flash floods.

For more information: Safford District Office, BLM, 425 East 4th St., Safford, AZ 85546, (602) 428-4040 or contact the BLM rangers at Aravaipa East (602) 828-3380 or Aravaipa West (602) 357-7111.

Permit: Obtain from BLM; limited in number and may be difficult to acquire for most weekends during warm months. Permit is required for overnight *and* day use. Length of stay is limited to three days and two nights. There is a fee of $1.50 per person per day. Pets are not permitted in the wilderness and horses are not permitted overnight in the canyon bottom.

All birds have keen eyesight, but turkey vultures are one of the few with a good sense of smell. After a hearty meal of carrion, vultures may have considerable difficulty taking off, but once in the air they search out rising thermals on which to soar effortlessly. From a distance, vultures can be distinguished from hawks by the way they hold their wings—hawks tend to hold their wings flat while gliding; vultures hold their wings at a slight angle or dihedral. Stewart Aitchison

By 1900, overgrazing by livestock and a slight change in the Southwest's rainfall pattern had turned many previously permanent desert streams into intermittent arroyos. The construction of dams on other rivers flooded canyons upstream and dried up the flood plains below the dams. Aravaipa Creek supports one of the last relatively intact desert riparian ecosystems and is a remarkable example of the diversity of desert life. Bruce Grubbs

Hikers can enter this 10-mile-long canyon from either side; however, the west entrance is easier to reach and thus more crowded. To reach the west entrance, turn off Arizona 77 onto Aravaipa Road 11 miles south of Winkleman. Take Aravaipa Road past Central Arizona College and proceed for 12 miles along this paved-and-dirt road until you reach the trailhead at a BLM parking lot and ranger station.

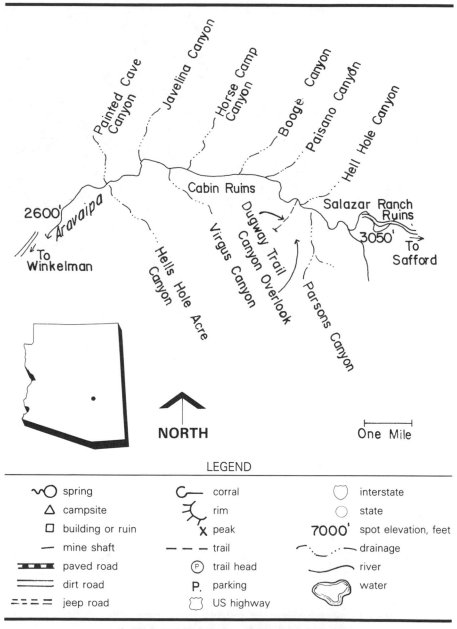

LEGEND

∿O	spring	C—	corral	◯	interstate
△	campsite	〒	rim	◯	state
□	building or ruin	X	peak	7000'	spot elevation, feet
—	mine shaft	– – –	trail	⌒·⌒	drainage
▰▰▰	paved road	Ⓟ	trail head	⌒⌒	river
═══	dirt road	P.	parking	◯	water
≡≡≡	jeep road	⬡	US highway		

ARAVAIPA CANYON HIKE 48

The east entrance requires a long drive on gravel roads. Turn off Arizona 70 about 8 miles southeast of Ft. Thomas and about 13 miles northwest of Safford, onto the Klondyke Road. Continue about 25 miles and turn right onto the Aravaipa Road, which takes you to Klondyke (about 9 miles from the junction), location of the BLM Ranger Station for the east entrance. Continue on for 10 miles through five stream crossings to reach the trailhead parking area. There is no trail as such; walking is simply *in* the shallow stream.

Aravaipa Canyon is unusual in that a permanent stream courses through its desert bottom. Sycamore, ash, cottonwood, and willow trees thrive along the creek. The abundance and diversity of wildlife is one of the many charms of this desert canyon. Eleven species of fish swim in the creek; more than fifty species of amphibians and reptiles are known to inhabit the area. Nearly fifty species of mammals have also been recorded here, from desert shrews to black bear. And, of course, the canyon is a birder's paradise with approximately two hundred species, including rare visits by the endangered peregrine falcon and Mexican species like rose-throated becards.

Evidence of prehistoric people is scattered throughout the Aravaipa region. Turkey Creek Canyon was a primary migration route of Indians, who lived and farmed near Aravaipa Creek.

Pioneers also tried to tame the canyon. Near the mouth of Horse Camp Canyon are the ruins of an unfinished cabin started about 1900. At Hell Hole Canyon is the original homestead of the Salazar family. The cave behind the remnants of the house was also once inhabited by settlers.

If time or energy is short, easy day hikes of 2 miles one way from either entrance will take you into scenic portions of the canyon.—*Tom Bean* □

HIKE 49 *CAMPAIGN CREEK-PINE CREEK LOOP*

General description: A three- or four-day loop hike in the Superstition Wilderness Area.
General location: Twenty miles northwest of Globe.
Maps: Pinyon Mountain 7.5-minute, Two Bar Mountain 7.5-minute, Haunted Canyon 7.5-minute, Iron Mountain 7.5-minute USGS quads; USFS Superstition Wilderness map.
Difficulty: Moderate.
Length: About 15 miles.
Elevation: 3,200 to 5,600 feet.
Special attractions: Permanent stream, historic ranches, pine forest, highest point in Superstition Mountains.
Water availability: See description.
Best season: October-November, March-May.
For more information: Mesa Ranger District, P.O. Drawer A, 26 N. MacDonald, Mesa, AZ 85201; (602) 261-6446.
Permit: None.

From Arizona 88, turn south onto Forest Road 449, approximately 7 miles east of Roosevelt Dam. Drive south on the main road about 7 miles to the signed trailhead, parking at the old Upper Horrel Place, a ranch which is now the Reavis Mountain School, a wilderness school. The trailhead area is privately owned; please stay on the trail. This approach road crosses Campaign Creek a number of times, and a high-clearance vehicle is advisable. The road may be impassable after a major storm.

By linking several trails, hikers can create a fine loop trip in the less-traveled, high, eastern end of the Superstition Mountains. Start by taking the signed Campaign Creek Trail (Forest Trail 256) from the trailhead less than .5 mile to the signed junction with the Reavis Gap Trail (Forest Trail 117). Take this trail west as it ascends a drainage system to Reavis Gap, a saddle at the south end of Two Bar Mountain. The area is open pinyon-juniper woodland with good views to the east. Walnut Spring, to the south on the Two Bar Ridge trail, is only a muddy seep. The Reavis Gap Trail ascends slightly over another ridge, then drops to cross Pine Creek in a stand of ponderosa pines. There is water here in the cool season and several fine campsites. Pine Creek is interesting to explore either up-or downstream.

Continuing west-southwest, the Reavis Gap Trail ascends another gradual slope to a pass, then descends to meet the signed Reavis Trail (Forest Trail 109) north of Reavis Ranch. Turn south on the Reavis Trail and follow Reavis Creek upstream about a mile to the old Reavis Ranch. Along the way, you will pass an old apple orchard which is so famous among hikers and horsepackers for its sweet fruit that it is picked clean every season.

Most people approach Reavis Ranch via the Reavis Trail, which used to be an access road to the ranch before it was sold to the Forest Service and became part of the wilderness area. The ranch site is becoming increasingly trashy and unpleasant as a campsite, but there is excellent camping above and below the ranch areas with water in the creek during the cool season.

In the Superstition Wilderness Area, Weaver's Needle is the site of the legendary Lost Dutchman Mine, where gold is hidden within the shadow of the needle. Despite the fact that the volcanic rock in the area has a very low potential for valuable minerals, "weekend prospectors" continue the search. Bruce Grubbs

Fish Creek Canyon in the heart of the Superstitions is easily reached by taking the Apache Trail Road. Since the canyon is trailless, you probably won't encounter very many people as you hike upstream. Bruce Grubbs

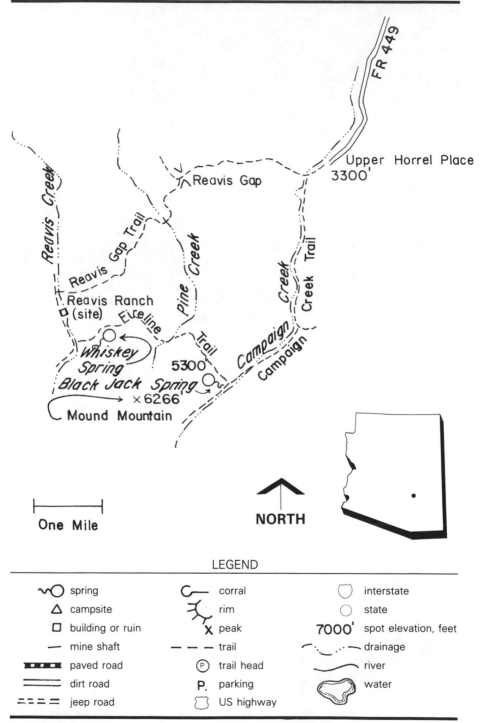

FR 449

Upper Horrel Place
3300'

Reavis Gap

Reavis Creek

Reavis Gap Trail

Pine Creek

Campaign Creek

Creek Trail

Reavis Ranch
(site)

Fireline

Whiskey
Spring

Black Jack Spring

Trail

5300

Campaign

Campaign

× 6266

Mound Mountain

One Mile

NORTH

LEGEND

∾○	spring	⊂	corral	◌	interstate	
△	campsite	⋔	rim	○	state	
☐	building or ruin	✕	peak	7000'	spot elevation, feet	
—	mine shaft	– – –	trail	⌒·⋯	drainage	
▮▮▮▮	paved road	Ⓟ	trail head		river	
═══	dirt road	P.	parking	⬭	water	
= = = =	jeep road	⬠	US highway			

CAMPAIGN CREEK-PINE CREEK LOOP HIKE 49

From Reavis Ranch, continue south on the Reavis Trail less than a mile to the signed junction with the Fireline Trail (Forest Trail 118), where you turn left (east) and ascend into a drainage. This trail is a former firebreak built to help contain a large fire which devastated the Mound Mountain-Iron Mountain area, probably in the 1950s. Despite the fire, the area still contains large stands of ponderosa pines, a surprise to people familiar only with the lower, western Superstitions.

The trail climbs past Whiskey Spring, which is probably reliable, then climbs steeply over the ridge and down into Pine Creek. From the ridge area, it is possible to hike cross-country to the summit of Mound Mountain, the highest point in the Superstition Mountains, without encountering too much brush. Indian ruins are common in this section of the Superstitions, and you will probably find one or more if you venture off-trail. Remember to leave them undisturbed for future hikers to enjoy.

There is limited camping and seasonal water at Pine Creek. The Fireline Trail continues down the creek for a short distance, then climbs over the ridge northeast of Mound Mountain and drops steeply into Campaign Creek to join the signed Campaign Creek Trail (Forest Trail 256). There is more camping here, and water during the cool season. For an enjoyable side hike, follow the Campaign Creek Trail south (right) to the saddle southwest of Pinto Peak, where fine vantage points survey the rugged Pinto Creek area.

Back at the junction with the Fireline Trail, continue north (left) on the Campaign Creek Trail as the creek gradually loses elevation and vegetation changes correspondingly. In the upper canyon, ponderosa pines are common; lower down, they are replaced by juniper and pinyon pine. Sycamores are abundant along the entire pleasant walk to the trailhead at Upper Horrel, and there are numerous places to camp.—*Bruce Grubbs* ☐

HIKE 50 *BULL PASTURE-MOUNT AJO*

General description: A round-trip day hike in the Organ Pipe Cactus National Monument Wilderness Area.
General location: Organ Pipe Cactus National Monument.
Maps: Mt. Ajo 15-minute USGS quad.
Difficulty: Moderate to difficult.
Length: About 3.5 miles one way.
Elevation: 2,300 to 4,800 feet.
Special attractions: Unique desert area, rugged mountains, historic ranching area.
Water availability: None.
Best season: October through April.
For more information: Organ Pipe Cactus National Monument, P.O. Box 38, Ajo, AZ 85321.
Permit: None for dayhikes.

From the Organ Pipe Cactus National Monument headquarters (a stop at the visitor center to learn about this unique desert area is worthwhile), take the Ajo Mountain loop drive to the signed Bull Pasture trailhead, about 8 miles.

The maintained trail leaves the picnic area and climbs about a mile to a ridge overlooking Bull Pasture, a scenic basin high on the flanks of the Ajo Range. Bull Pasture was a favorite cow pasture back in the days when grazing was still allowed in the area. From the trail's end at the overlook, a rough but rewarding cross-country hike leads to the summit of Mount Ajo, at 4,808 feet the highest in the monument. Leave the end of the trail and work your way around the head of the Bull Pasture basin, moving generally east toward the steep slopes on the far side. Then head generally up and right to gain the main north-south ridgecrest. You will have to pick your way around some cliff bands. Once you have reached the ridge, it is a straightforward walk north about a mile to the summit, your turnaround point.

From the ridge and the summit, you can see far south into Mexico, west across Organ Pipe Cactus National Monument, and north and east across the Papago Indian Reservation toward rugged Baboquivari Mountain. This rugged basin-and-range topography is typical of southwest Arizona.—*Bruce Grubbs* □

Hedgehog cactus is one of the earlist blooming cacti; the lavender-to-tich-red flowers appear as early as March. The dark red, juicy fruits of the hedgehog cactus are eaten by birds and rodents, and the Pima Indians consider them a delicacy. Stewart Aitchison

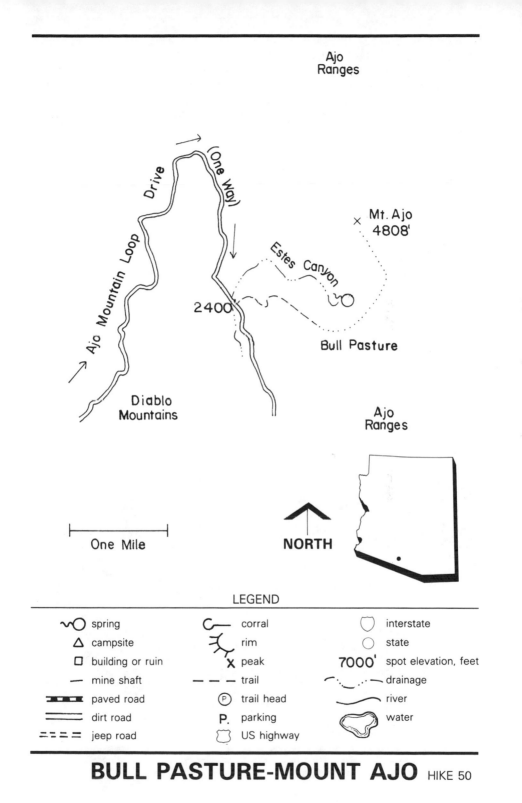

Ajo
Ranges

Ajo Mountain Loop Drive

(One Way)

× Mt. Ajo
4808'

Estes Canyon

2400

Bull Pasture

Diablo
Mountains

Ajo
Ranges

One Mile

NORTH

LEGEND

~⊙ spring	C— corral	◯ interstate
△ campsite	rim	◯ state
▢ building or ruin	× peak	**7000'** spot elevation, feet
— mine shaft	– – – trail	drainage
paved road	Ⓟ trail head	river
dirt road	P. parking	water
=== jeep road	US highway	

BULL PASTURE-MOUNT AJO HIKE 50

General description: A moderate round-trip day hike (which may be extended) in the Pusch Ridge Wilderness Area.

General location: Coronado National Forest, northwest of Tucson.

Maps: Mt. Lemmon 15-minute USGS quad; Southern Arizona Hiking Club's Santa Catalina map.

Difficulty: Moderate.

Length: 7.2 miles one-way to Mt. Lemmon Trail.

Elevation: 2,800 to 6,000 feet.

Special attractions: Beautiful vistas, solitude, waterfalls, and slickrock areas; vegetation from Sonoran desert to coniferous forests, all within a short distance of Tucson.

Water availability: Unreliable and quality questionable; pack your own.

Best season: October to May; summer is unbearably hot.

For more information: Santa Catalina Ranger District, Rt. 15, Box 277F, Tucson, AZ 85715; (602) 629-5113.

Permit: None—however, there is an entry fee at the entrance station to Catalina State Park.

To find the trailhead, go north on Oracle Road approximately 6 miles from the Ina intersection. Turn right into Catalina State Park (where a nominal entry fee is required) and continue to the Day Use Area. Park here and walk across the streambed just southeast of the information center. Trails are marked and a map of the park area is available at the entrance station.

An unusual cristate form of saguaro cactus, this fan-shaped condition is an abnormal growth resulting from an injury at the apex caused by fungi, bacteria, birds, or insects. Round holes are sometimes seen near the tops of branches. These have usually been made by Gila woodpeckers or flickers for nests. Afterwards these cavitities may be occupied by elf owls. Stewart Aitchison

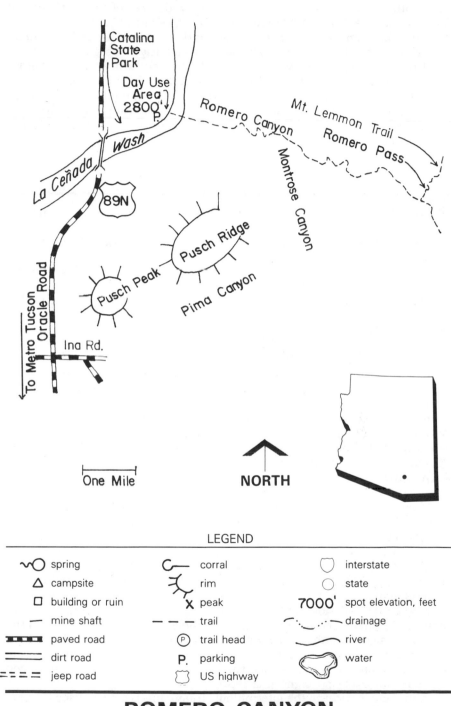

Catalina
State
Park

Day Use
Area
2800'
P.

Romero Canyon

Mt. Lemmon Trail

Romero Pass

La Ceñada Wash

89N

Montrose Canyon

Pusch Peak

Pusch Ridge

Pima Canyon

To Metro Tucson
Oracle Road

Ina Rd.

One Mile

NORTH

LEGEND

∿○	spring	C⌒	corral	⬡	interstate
△	campsite	⋎	rim	○	state
☐	building or ruin	X	peak	**7000'**	spot elevation, feet
—	mine shaft	– – –	trail	⌒‥⌒	drainage
▰▰▰	paved road	Ⓟ	trail head		river
═══	dirt road	P.	parking	▱	water
≡≡≡	jeep road	⬡	US highway		

ROMERO CANYON HIKE 51

This trail will give you access to the major north-south region of the Santa Catalina Mountains, just north of Tucson. It also provides access to many other trails within the area (such as Mt. Lemmon, Wilderness of Rocks, Cathedral Rock, Canada Del Oro, and Sutherland, among others). The trail is marked at the trailhead and continues to be well-marked, at least as far as the junction with the Mt. Lemmon Trail. It maintains a fairly steep grade but is not tortuous, and hikers can always shorten the trip by turning around before reaching the turnaround point at the Mt. Lemmon Trail intersection.

The hiking in this area is rewarding and dramatic. Many flowers bloom in the spring and you can expect to find water in the main canyons. By summer, though, the water is gone. This trail offers a great respite from the hustle and bustle of the city and excellent access to more remote areas.—*Bill Williams* □

HIKE 52 *PIMA CANYON*

General description: A round-trip day hike into the Pusch Ridge Wilderness Area.

General location: Just north of Tucson city limits, near the Ina Road-Oracle Road intersection.

Maps: Mt. Lemmon 15-minute USGS quad; Southern Arizona Hiking Club's Santa Catalina map.

Difficulty: Moderate.

Length: 7.6 miles to junction with Kimball Trail.

Elevation: 2,900 to 7,200 feet.

Special attractions: Wilderness solitude within a short distance of the Tucson metro area; flowing stream from winter through spring; beautiful desert riparian habitat.

Water availability: Unreliable and of questionable quality.

Best season: October to May; summer too hot.

For more information: Santa Catalina Ranger District, Rt. 15, Box 277F, Tucson, AZ 85715; (602) 629-5113.

Permit: None.

Although the trailhead is only a few minutes drive from downtown Tucson, within fifteen minutes of hiking you are isolated from the city. The trail is well-marked and popular, providing wonderful views of the Sonoran Desert.

To locate the trailhead, drive north on Oracle Road a mile from the Ina-Oracle intersection and then turn right onto Magee Road. Drive to the end of Magee Road (about 1.5 miles) and follow the signed, major trail (Forest Trail 62) eastward toward the mouth of Pima Canyon. The trail enters the canyon on the left side of the streambed, then meanders up the canyon, crossing the streambed many times. Nevertheless, it is easy to follow all the way to the signed Kimball Trail junction, your turnaround point. The length of your trip up Pima Canyon is only limited by your desire and time. During the winter months, there is a wide variety of birdlife in the area. Also, keep a lookout for deer and bighorn sheep.

When there is water in the intermittent stream, this is a great place to enjoy the warm weather. This day hike ends at the junction with Forest Trail 42.

From that junction, however, a number of other trails lead into the wilderness area, any of which allow for longer backpack trips into the higher, coniferous forests and provide great views.—*Bill Williams* □

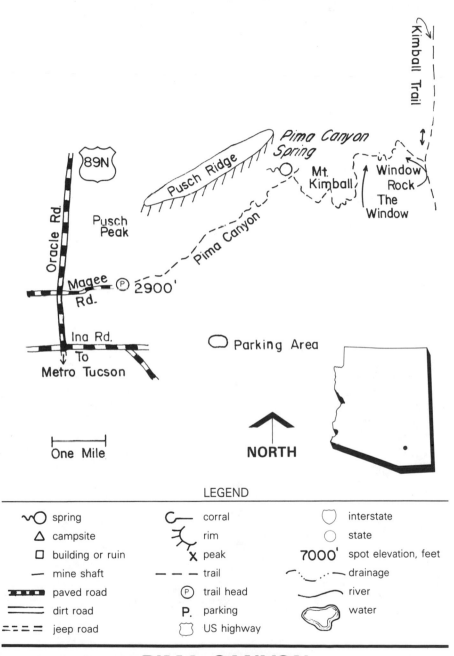

Parking Area

One Mile

NORTH

LEGEND

∿⃝ spring	Ⳅ corral	⃝ interstate	
△ campsite	⤙ rim	⃝ state	
☐ building or ruin	✗ peak	**7000'** spot elevation, feet	
— mine shaft	– – – trail	⌢‥⌣ drainage	
▰▰▰ paved road	ⓟ trail head	⌢⌣ river	
═══ dirt road	P. parking	⬮ water	
≡≡≡ jeep road	⬠ US highway		

PIMA CANYON HIKE 52

HIKE 53 *MICA MOUNTAIN*

General description: An overnight, round-trip backpack on the main trail to the highest point of the Rincon Mountains in the Saguaro National Monument Wilderness Area.

General location: Trailhead is at the east end of Speedway Boulevard in Tucson.

Maps: Rincon Valley 15-minute USGS quad; Southern Arizona Hiking Club's Rincons map.

Difficulty: Moderate; good, well-marked trail.

Length: From the end of Speedway to the tower on Mica Mountain is 12.4 miles one way.

Elevation: 2,748 to 8,666 feet.

Special attractions: The only high mountain range left in Arizona which is not topped by a road; wonderful wilderness.

Water availability: Permanent water only at Italian Springs and Manning Camp. Douglas Springs (5 miles from the trailhead) have seasonal water except in late spring and late fall.

The desert bighorn sheep is more dependent on water than many desert mammals. Therefore one of the best places to observe them is at a spring or a natural rock tank called tinajas in southern Arizona. They try to drink at least once a day, usually in the early morning. Stewart Aitchison

Best season: Spring, fall, winter; summer temperatures can be brutal.
For more information: Saguaro National Monument, Old Spanish Trail, Route 8, Box 695, Tucson, AZ 85730; (602) 296-8576.
Permit: Required for overnight use. Camping only in designated campgrounds: Douglas Springs and Manning Camp. No pets or firearms allowed.

Since no hunting is allowed in the Monument, it abounds with wildlife. It is not uncommon for quiet hikers to see deer, javelina, or coyotes.

For purposes of this hike description, the Mica Mountain Trail can be divided into three segments, each with an elevation gain of about 2,000 feet. From the end of Speedway to Douglas Springs, the vegetation typifies the Sonoran Desert. The trail climbs 2,000 feet in about 3 miles and then remains fairly level for the next 2 miles. Hikers may want to take a nice side trip to a waterfall about 1.5 miles from the trailhead—as you enter a mesquite thicket, the falls can be seen on the right. Where the map shows "Aquila Corral," a well-used horse trail leads to the fall's base.

From Douglas Spring, the trail climbs to Cowhead Saddle. About a mile from the campground, you enter a lovely forested canyon. If you are low on water, this is the last place to fill up before reaching the top—a small, stagnant pool, but still better than being without.

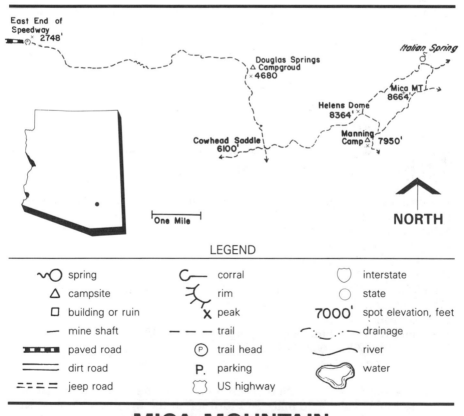

LEGEND

∿O	spring	C—	corral	⬭	interstate
△	campsite	⅄	rim	◯	state
☐	building or ruin	✗	peak	**7000'**	spot elevation, feet
—	mine shaft	– – –	trail	⌐‿·‿	drainage
▰▰▰	paved road	Ⓟ	trail head	‿‿	river
═══	dirt road	P.	parking	⬡	water
= = = =	jeep road	⬡	US highway		

MICA MOUNTAIN   HIKE 53

As you climb out of the canyon, the Cowhead (which looks more like a sitting camel) is directly in front of you. From a trail intersection at the saddle, take the trail to Mica, which climbs on the ridge to the east.

Just when the ridge seems like it will never end, the trail turns and drops into a beautiful drainage forested with ponderosa pines. The trail continues up the drainage, past a huge rock outcropping on the left—Helen's Dome—and to a fork.

At the fork you can relax. You are now only a couple hundred feet lower than the top, your turnaround point. You also have a choice of which way to go to Mica.

The North Slope Trail goes through lush vegetation for 2 miles until it comes to Italian Springs, a permanent source of water. From the spring, it climbs south to join another trail. Going east on this trail will take you to Mica Secondary. The view from here is worth the few minutes it takes to climb it.

Heading back west, the trail goes to Mica Tower. The view from the tower is superb. Unfortunately, since the tower is no longer in use, the Park Service has enclosed the base with barbed wire and has removed the lower stairs.

There is also an easier route to Mica from the fork near Helen's Dome. Take the trail to the south, which leads to Manning Camp. After .2 mile, there is an another fork. From here to the tower is only 1.4 miles. This trail goes by Spud Rock, which is only a few feet lower than Mica. Again the view is worth the short, easy scramble.

There is no register at the summit, but there is one at Manning Camp. A nice loop hike also follows the trail east from the tower for about .1 mile. The trail coming from the southwest takes you right to Manning.

The cabin at Manning Camp was built by Arizona pioneer Levi Manning as a summer home in 1905. Reportedly, Mrs. Manning had a piano in it. Today, it is used only by Park Service personnel. There is water throughout the year in the little lake near the cabin.—*Sid Hirsh* □

HIKE 54 *SYCAMORE CANYON*

General description: A round-trip day hike into the Pajarita Wilderness Area.
General location: Fifteen miles west of Nogales.
Maps: Ruby 7.5-minute USGS quad; Coronado National Forest map.
Difficulty: Moderate.
Length: About 6 miles one way.
Elevation: 3,500 to 4,000 feet.
Special attractions: A botanist's and birder's paradise.
Water availability: Permanent stream.
Best season: All year.
For more information: Nogales Ranger District, 2480 Tucson-Nogales Hwy., Nogales, AZ 85621; (602) 281-2296.
Permit: None.

Drive about 55 miles south of Tucson on Interstate 19 and then exit onto Arizona 289. Go about 20 miles and turn left at the Sycamore Canyon sign. The parking area is .5 mile down this road at Hank and Yank Spring, the site

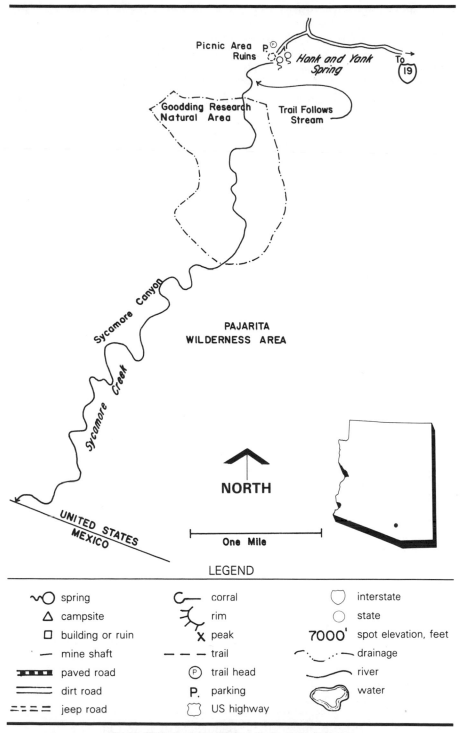

Picnic Area
Ruins
P Ⓒ

Hank and Yank
Spring

To 19

Goodding Research
Natural Area

Trail Follows
Stream

Sycamore Canyon

Sycamore Creek

PAJARITA
WILDERNESS AREA

UNITED STATES
MEXICO

NORTH

One Mile

LEGEND

∿◯	spring	Ⅽ—	corral	◯	interstate
△	campsite	⅄	rim	◯	state
▢	building or ruin	✗	peak	7000'	spot elevation, feet
—	mine shaft	– – –	trail	⌣·⌣··⌣	drainage
▮▮▮▮	paved road	Ⓟ	trail head	⌒	river
═══	dirt road	P.	parking	◌	water
≡≡≡	jeep road	⬠	US highway		

SYCAMORE CANYON HIKE 54

of an old post-Civil War ranch that was founded by Hank Hewitt and Yank Bartlett.

There is no "official" trail but rather just a route going downstream. To avoid wading, especially at high water, you may have to do some fancy footwork along cliffs and ledges. Avoid this route, however, if there is any chance of flooding.

This pleasant walk along the streambed eventually ends at the Mexican border, some 6 miles distant, marked by an old barbed wire fence. There are a number of swimming holes to divert your attention.

The stream is home to a rare desert fish called the Sonoran chub. But don't break out your fishing pole. These fish are usually no more than four inches long and, besides, are protected by law.

Part of the canyon has been set aside as the Goodding Research Natural Area. Botanists have identified more than 624 species of plants in the Sycamore Canyon area; many of them are rare and endangered. Several have disjointed ranges,' which means that they are found only in scattered, isolated populations. One of the more intriguing such species is a fern which exists only in the Himalayas, Mexico, and here at Sycamore Canyon.

In addition to rare species, sycamores and Arizona walnuts thrive along the creek and juniper and oak dot drier slopes. A few saguaro stand on the warmer, south-facing slopes. Look for western coral-bean, a large shrub with light brown bark containing longitudinal white lines. The bright red seeds of the western coral-bean are poisonous, and in Mexico are strung together to make necklaces.

Birders will have a marvelous time along this creek, especially in spring and summer. Black phoebe, vermilion flycatcher, red-tailed hawk, common black-hawk, several kinds of herons, and woodpeckers are only a few of more than 130 species of birds that frequent the area.

Hikers also may encounter coatimundis. These Mexican relatives of the raccoon often congregate in bands of a dozen individuals or more and are most active during the day. They are omnivorous, with a tough nose pad which aids in rooting for grubs and tubers. Included in their diet are fruits, nuts, bird eggs, lizards, scorpions and tarantulas.—*Stewart Aitchison, John Nelson, Dale Shewalter* □

HIKE 55 *MOUNT WRIGHTSON*

General description: A round-trip day hike into the Mount Wrightson Wilderness Area.

General location: Thirty-five miles south of Tucson.

Maps: Mount Wrightson 15-minute USGS quad; Coronado National Forest map.

Difficulty: Difficult.

Length: About 6.5 miles one way.

Elevation: 5,400 to 9,453 feet.

Special attractions: Fantastic birding, great vistas.

Water availability: Sprung Spring, Bellows Spring, and Baldy Spring may be dry.

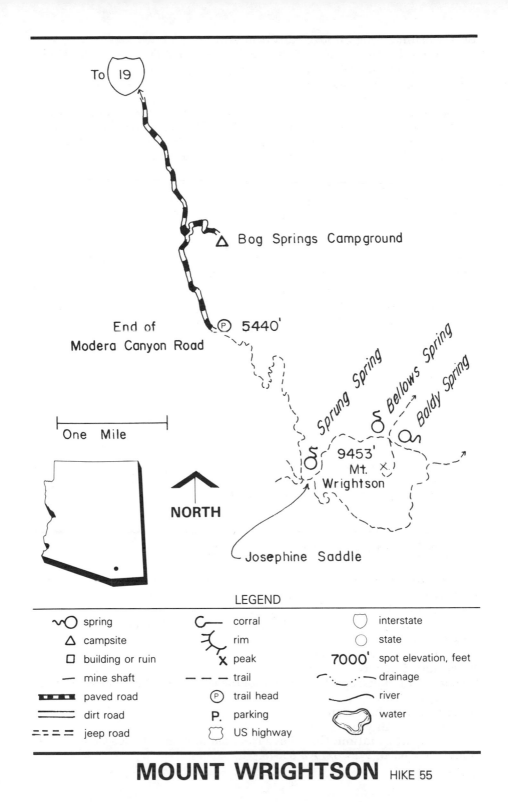

To ⬡ 19

△ Bog Springs Campground

End of
Modera Canyon Road

℗ 5440'

Sprung Spring

Bellows Spring

Baldy Spring

One Mile

NORTH

9453'
Mt. ✕
Wrightson

Josephine Saddle

LEGEND

∿◯ spring	⌒ corral	◯ interstate
△ campsite	rim	◯ state
▢ building or ruin	✕ peak	**7000'** spot elevation, feet
— mine shaft	– – – trail	drainage
paved road	℗ trail head	river
dirt road	P. parking	water
≡≡≡ jeep road	⬡ US highway	

MOUNT WRIGHTSON HIKE 55

Best season: Spring through early winter.
For more information: Nogales Ranger District, 2480 Tucson-Nogales Hwy., Nogales, AZ 85621; (602) 281-2296.
Permit: None.

Drive south from Tucson on Interstate 19. About 4 miles south of Green Valley, exit the Interstate onto the Continental/Madera Canyon Road. Follow the signs to the upper end of Madera Canyon and the Roundup Picnic Area parking lot. The trail (Forest Trail 134) begins at the north end of the parking area.

This hike begins by following a tributary of Madera Canyon. Here in the riparian habitat of walnut, sycamore, and velvet ash, you may see solitary vireo, acorn woodpeckers, Mexican jays, black-headed grosbeaks, red-shafted flickers, western tanagers, sulphur-bellied flycatchers, yellow-eyed juncos, and the rare elegant trogon. More than 170 species of birds have been recorded in this area. The trail crosses the creek and ascends through silverleaf oaks, Arizona white oaks, Emory oaks, Arizona madrone, and alligator junipers.

Just before reaching Josephine Saddle, where three Boy Scouts died of hypothermia in November of 1958, you encounter unreliable Sprung Spring. Turn left at the saddle onto Forest Trail 78, go about a .25 mile and turn left again onto Forest Trail 94. The right fork (Forest Trail 78) is a longer but less steep route to the summit.

You soon come to Bellows Spring, which may be dry. The trail proceeds up to Baldy Saddle. From the saddle head south. The route climbs through Mexican white pine and Douglas fir and finally switchbacks to the open summit. You are treated to terrific views of the Santa Ritas and surrounding desert. The Mount Hopkins telescope is visible to the west.

You can return by taking the trail (Forest Trail 78) that goes around the east and south side of the mountain and intersects your ascent route just before reaching Josephine Saddle. Baldy Spring, located along this section, is about as reliable as the other springs. Check with the Forest Service before relying on these water sources.—*Stewart Aitchison*

HIKE 56   *SUGARLOAF MOUNTAIN*

General description: A round-trip day hike to one of the highest viewpoints in the Chiricahua National Monument Wilderness Area.
General location: One hundred miles east of Tucson.
Maps: Cochise Head 7.5-minute USGS quad; National Monument brochure.
Difficulty: Easy.
Length: One mile one way.
Elevation: 6,800 to 7,305 feet.
Special attractions: Spectacular view of the Chiricahua National Monument Wilderness Area.
Water availability: None.
Best season: All year.
For more information: Chiricahua National Monument, Dos Cabezas Star Route, Box 6500, Willcox, AZ 85643.
Permit: None.

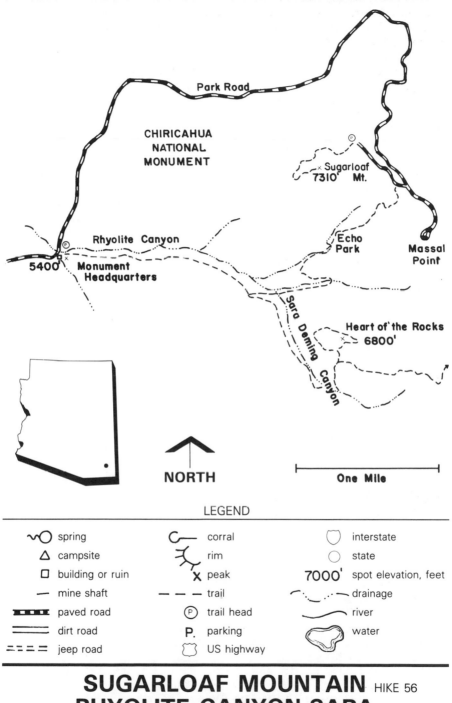

Park Road

CHIRICAHUA
NATIONAL
MONUMENT

× Sugarloaf
7310' Mt.

Rhyolite Canyon

5400
Monument
Headquarters

Echo
Park

Massal
Point

Sara Deming Canyon

Heart of the Rocks
× 6800'

NORTH

One Mile

LEGEND

∿○	spring	C	corral	⬡	interstate
△	campsite	⨇	rim	○	state
☐	building or ruin	✗	peak	7000'	spot elevation, feet
—	mine shaft	– – –	trail	⌒⋯⌒	drainage
▰▰▰	paved road	Ⓟ	trail head	⌒	river
═══	dirt road	P.	parking	⬭	water
= = =	jeep road	⬡	US highway		

SUGARLOAF MOUNTAIN HIKE 56
RHYOLITE CANYON-SARA
DEMING CANYON HIKE 57

Turn south off of Interstate 10 at the Willcox exit some 80 miles east of Tucson. From here, Arizona 186 winds through the old section of Willcox and then travels southeast for 30 miles to the monument entrance.

An alternate route on the east side of the Chiricahuas goes through the town of Portal. Turn off of U.S. 80 and follow Forest Road 42 over the mountains to the monument entrance. This road is occasionally blocked by snow during the winter.

The Chiricahuas are on a par with Bryce and Zion canyons for the beauty and spectacular nature of their geology. Your drive from the monument entrance to the trailhead takes you through lush Bonita Canyon and ascends toward Massai Point. Approximately 5.5 miles from the monument headquarters is a turn-off to the Sugarloaf Mountain parking area.

Your trail is visible from the upper parking lot, and leads a mile to the top of Sugarloaf, your turnaround point, which offers an incredible view of the monument and the surrounding area. On all sides are the sculpted and fractured volcanic rhyolite formations that the Chiricahuas are famous for.

The monument boasts seven different varieties of oak, as well as pines, cypress, fir, and juniper. The Chiricahuas are the northern limit for many plants and animals otherwise endemic to Mexico. Mixed with woodlands are yuccas, agave, and sotols. Javelina are quite common, as are whitetail deer. Many birds breed in or migrate through the monument, including a number of hummingbirds and exotic species such as the rose-throated becard and elegant trogon.

This area was one of the strongholds for Geronimo's band of Chiricahua Apaches. Fort Bowie is a short drive from the monument, and the National Park Service has a small interpretive station at the remains of the old fort.— *Steve Gustafson* □

HIKE 57 *RHYOLITE CANYON-SARA DEMING CANYON*

General description: A round-trip day hike into the Chiricahua National Monument Wilderness Area.
General location: One hundred miles east of Tucson.
Maps: Cochise Head 7.5-minute USGS quad; National Monument brochure.
Difficulty: Moderate.
Length: About 3 miles one way to the Heart of the Rocks area.
Elevation: 5,400 to 6,800 feet.
Special attractions: Strange rock formations and abundant wildlife.
Water availability: None.
Best season: All year.
For more information: Chiricahua National Monument, Dos Cabezas Star Route, Box 6500, Willcox, AZ 85643; (602) 824-3560.
Permit: None.

This trail begins at the Chiricahua National Monument visitor center parking lot. It climbs out of lower Bonita Canyon into the upper reaches of Rhyolite Canyon. At the 1.5-mile point, take the right fork, the Sara Deming Canyon Trail. Another 1.5 miles brings you to the Heart of the Rocks area, a land of strange balanced rocks and fanciful shapes. A signed one-mile-long trail loops through the Heart of the Rocks, which you may want to take before heading back.

These unusual rock formations are carved out of rhyolite, a type of rock formed when white-hot volcanic ash piles up in layers and welds itself together. Later mountain uplifting caused the rhyolite to fracture into definite patterns. Along the vertical cracks and planes of horizontal weakness, erosion by weathering and running water began to shape the rock into the formations we see today.—*Chiricahua National Monument* □

HIKE 58 *CHIRICAHUA PEAK*

General description: An overnight round-trip backpack to the summit of the Chiricahua Wilderness Area (which is different from the Chiricahua National Monument Wilderness Area named in the previous two hike descriptions).
General location: One hundred miles east of Tucson.
Maps: Chiricahua Peak 15-minute USGS quad; Coronado National Forest map.
Difficulty: Difficult.
Length: About 7 miles one way.
Elevation: 6,300 to 9,796 feet.
Special attractions: Possible sightings of mountain lions; Mexican wolves; Rocky Mountain, Sonoran, and Chihuahuan species of birds.

The remarkable rhyolite pillars in the Chiricahua National Monument Wilderness Area are the result of fused volcanic ash being eroded into columns. At least eight eruptions are responsible for the accumulation of nearly two thousand feet of volcanic ash, also called tuff. Stewart Aitchison.

Water availability: Anita Spring is usually running.
Best season: Spring through fall.
For more information: Douglas Ranger District, Rt. 1, Box 228R, Leslie Canyon Road, Douglas, AZ 85607; (602) 364-3468.
Permit: None.

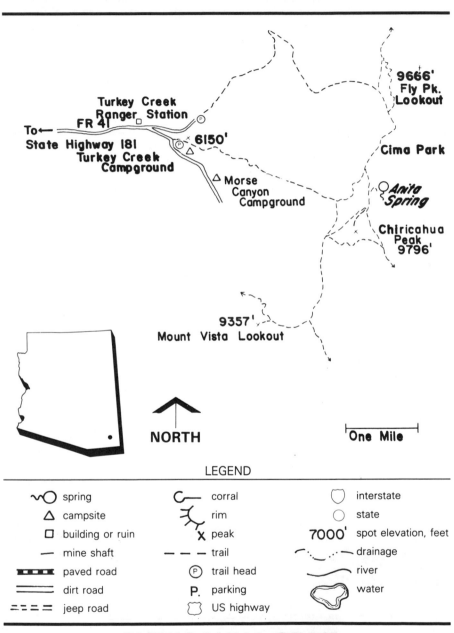

CHIRICAHUA PEAK HIKE 58

To reach this wonderful hike, drive about 70 miles east of Tucson on Interstate 10. Exit at U.S. 666 and head south 25 miles to Arizona 181. Drive east on 181 about 12 miles and turn onto Forest Road 41. Nine miles will bring you to a signed, short spur road to the Saulsbury Canyon Trail (Forest Trail 263).

The trail begins by ambling up through a lovely forest of oak, Apache and Chihuahua pine, and Arizona cypress. The route steepens, but you are treated to magnificent views across the wilderness and Sulphur Springs Valley. As you continue to climb, the vegetation will change to Douglas fir and Engelmann spruce and finally some quaking aspen.

Turn right at the signed Crest Trail (Forest Trail 270) and walk south toward Round Park. Water is usually available at Booger Springs, although it may be dry in a drought year. Farther south you come to Anita Park and Anita Spring, which like Booger Spring may be dry. Otherwise this is a good campsite.

From Anita Park, it is another mile to the summit of Chiricahua Peak, your turnaround point. Unfortunately, the dense forest blocks most of the view.

This area does not have the strange rock formations found in the nearby Chiricahua National Monument, but the amazing variety of plants and wildlife should satisfy any naturalist. Mexican wolves are known to occasionally enter the area and there are persistent rumors of Mexican grizzlies. There are definitely black bear and mountain lion in this range.

Many birds utilize this area, not only typical Arizona and Mexican species but also some Eastern species such as warblers passing through on their migrations to and from Mexico.—*Stewart Aitchison* □

HIKE 59 *WABAYUMA PEAK*

General description: A round-trip day hike to the top of 7,601-foot Wabayuma Peak.
General location: Thirty miles southeast of Kingman in the Hualapai Mountains.
Maps: Wabayuma Peak 7.5-minute USGS quad.
Difficulty: Moderate with some cross-country travel.
Length: About 3 miles one way.
Elevation: 6,047 to 7,601 feet.
Special attractions: Spectacular views of the nearby mountain ranges and the Mohave Desert.
Water availability: None.
Best season: Late spring through fall.
For more information: Kingman Resource Area, Bureau of Land Management, 2475 Beverly Avenue, Kingman, AZ 86401; (602) 757-3161.
Permit: None.
Wilderness status: BLM Wilderness Study Area.

Wabayuma Peak is the second-tallest peak in the Hualapai Mountain Range. The mountains were named after the Hualapai Indians, the people of the tall pines, a Yuman Indian group who used to live in the nearby valleys and along

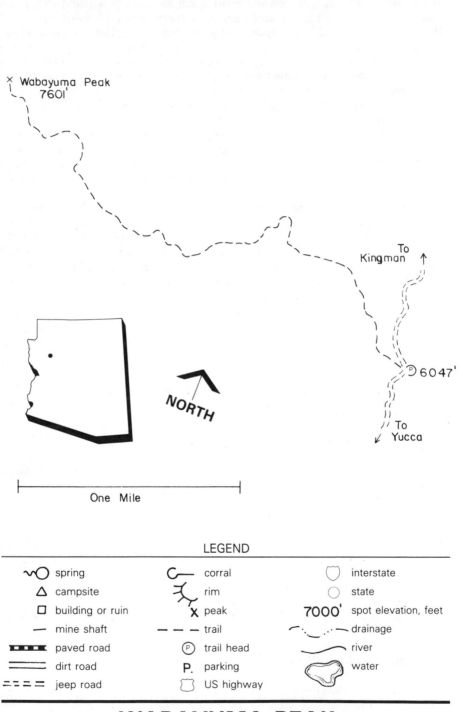

× Wabayuma Peak
7601'

To
Kingman

6047'

To
Yucca

NORTH

One Mile

LEGEND

∿○	spring	C	corral	◠	interstate	
△	campsite	⋔	rim	○	state	
☐	building or ruin	X	peak	**7000'**	spot elevation, feet	
—	mine shaft	– – –	trail	⌇	drainage	
▪▪▪▪	paved road	Ⓟ	trail head	〰	river	
═══	dirt road	P.	parking	◯	water	
═ ═ ═	jeep road	⬔	US highway			

WABAYUMA PEAK HIKE 59

a portion of the lower Colorado River. The steep but fairly easy hike to the top of this peak rewards hikers with expansive views of the surrounding country. There is no water source on this trail, so bring enough.

The biggest struggle on this hike is getting to the trailhead. A four-wheel-drive vehicle is recommended. Snow may block the northern approach road until late spring.

To reach the trailhead, follow the Hualapai Mountain Road out of Kingman. Drive through Hualapai Mountain County Park and past the recently built houses. Leave the pavement after 12.6 miles, turning right onto the dirt road. The small wooden signs for Flag Mine Road and Wild Cow Springs mark your turn. In another 3.7 miles, you reach Wild Cow Spring campground. The road continues through the campground and then climbs steeply up the hill. Stay on the main road that follows the ridgeline to the south for another 13.5 miles. Park at the shallow pullout opposite the jeep trail that takes off steeply up the hill to the northwest. The trailhead is 29.8 miles from the start of the Hualapai Mountain Road.

A shorter but much rougher approach leaves Interstate 40 at the Alamo Road in Yucca. After 1.4 miles, turn left on the Borianna Mine Road. Follow this rocky road up the Copper Creek drainage, past the relic Borianna Mine (at mile 17.3), up the steep grade, and along the ridge for another 3 miles.

The first 2 miles of your hiking trail follow an old jeep road that is blocked by a fallen tree. Manzanita, shrub live oak, and banana yucca line the trail. This warmer, southern exposure is a major influence on the types of plants that grow here. After the initial climb, the trail crosses some cooler, shaded pockets. An immediate transition to ponderosa pine trees occurs. As the trail heads west, good views of Hualapai Peak to the north appear. The rocky outcrop of Wabayuma Peak is visible to the west.

After approximately 2 miles, the jeep track drops down into a small clearing and then makes a sharp bend to the north. A short stretch of fence line on your left as the trail descends is your other guidemark. At this bend look for a narrow trail heading northwest up the shrub-filled slope. Two small cairns mark the start of this final ascent.

The trail switchbacks quickly up the slope; pink and yellow rocks serve as steps along the way. Deer use is evident on the trail. When the trail enters a grove of ponderosa pine, notched blaze marks keep you on track.

As the trail crosses the saddle and starts to descend, it is time to head cross-country. The exposed rocky point to the south is only four feet lower than the summit, but it is a much easier scramble. The second peak visible to the north is the actual summit of Wabayuma Peak. After bushwacking, a steep rock climb will put you on top. Hedgehog cactus are growing in the cracks of the rocks, so careful placement of hands and feet is essential for a safe ascent.

From the top, spectacular views of the Black Mountains to the west, Hualapai Peak to the north, the Aquarius Montains to the east, and the rest of the Hualapai Mountains to the south reward your climb. Return the way you came.—*Rudi Lambrechtse* □

HIKE 60 *PALM CANYON*

General description: A round-trip day hike to a desert oasis.
General location: Twenty-two miles southeast of Quartzite.
Maps: Livingston Hills 15-minute USGS quad.
Difficulty: Easy (cross-country).
Length: .75 mile one way.
Elevation: 2,100 to 2,500 feet.
Special attractions: Native palm trees growing in a desert canyon oasis.
Water availability: None.
Best season: All year, but very hot in summer.
For more information: Kofa National Wildlife Refuge, P.O. Box 1032, Yuma, AZ 85364.
Permit: None.
Wilderness status: FWS Wilderness Study Area.

To reach Palm Canyon drive either 19 miles south of Quartzite or 62 miles north of Yuma on Arizona 95. Turn off onto a signed dirt road that heads east toward the Kofa Range. At the Kofa National Wildlife Refuge boundary you may pick up a brochure describing the area.

A .75-mile walk up the wash at the end of the road will bring you to the palms. These are California Washingtonia palms. In Arizona, they only occur in Palm Canyon and in other deep, narrow canyons of the Kofa Mountains. Also keep watch for bighorn sheep.

Today the species is commonly planted as an ornamental in southern Arizona, but this native population was not discovered until 1923. In southeastern California, where this species is more common, the fruits were gathered and eaten by Indians. The botanist who named this palm dedicated it to President George Washington.

In the 1890s, Charles Eichelberger discovered the King of Arizona Mine in this rugged range. To mark company property, he had a branding iron that read "K of A." Later when a post office name was being discussed, someone remembered the brand and the name Kofa resulted.—*Stewart Aitchison* □

The rugged Kofa Mountains offer refuge for the desert bighorn sheep. Bruce Grubbs

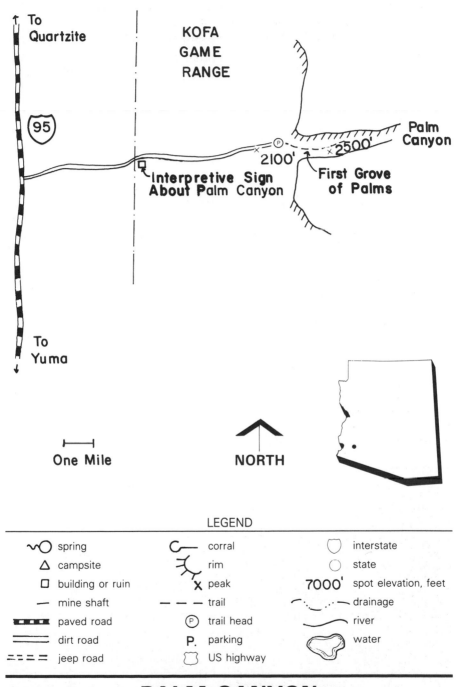

To
Quartzite

KOFA
GAME
RANGE

Palm
Canyon

95

2500'

2100'

Interpretive Sign
About Palm Canyon

First Grove
of Palms

To
Yuma

One Mile

NORTH

LEGEND

⌒O	spring	C⌒	corral	⬡	interstate
△	campsite		rim	◯	state
▢	building or ruin	X	peak	7000'	spot elevation, feet
—	mine shaft	– – –	trail	⌢⋯⌢	drainage
▮▮▮▮	paved road	Ⓟ	trail head	⌒	river
══	dirt road	P.	parking	⬭	water
≡≡≡	jeep road	⌒	US highway		

PALM CANYON HIKE 60

AFTERWORD

Arizona's wilderness challenge

Arizona is a land of many wild places. Its snow-covered peaks, lush canyons, and pristine deserts call out to us. There is, perhaps, no other place in the lower 48 states where one can better experience the grandeur and raw beauty of wilderness. It is for this reason that so many of us choose to visit or live in Arizona.

The lure of wilderness is an important part of the western mystique. The American West was a symbol of hope for the brave and adventurous. It was a place that rewarded the strong and self-reliant. It was a place where you could "get away" from the negative qualities of civilized life. And most important, it was a place where you could be free. The Wild West is gone, but the dream it represents lingers in our western wildernesses.

We are not the only ones who need or use those wild places. There are thousands of plant and animal species which make up the natural environment, plants and animals which evolved through the ages into an intricate web of life. It is their world we visit when we enter the wilderness; it is their natural order that many of us find so appealing and perplexing.

However, these wild lands are disappearing. Arizona is now one of the fastest-growing states in the country. As our numbers increase, so do our demands for more housing, farms, mines, roads, and similar developments. Something has to give. That something is too often the natural environment.

The solution is to set aside a few wild places now. This is not a new idea. President Theodore Roosevelt started a tradition of conservation with the creation of Grand Canyon National Monument in 1908 (congress made it a park in 1919) the first of many national parks in Arizona. The Forest Service pondered the idea of wilderness for another forty years. In 1964, Congress adopted the Wilderness Act and officially designated certain lands as parts of a national wilderness system. In 1976, Congress passed the Organic Act, a similar mechanism, so that Bureau of Land Management lands can also be designated wilderness.

So where are we now? There are only about 2 million acres of designated wilderness in Arizona—less than 3 percent of our state. Nearly half of this acreage was added in the 1984 Arizona Wilderness Bill, which primarily affected Forest Service lands statewide and BLM lands within the Arizona Strip country north of the Colorado River.

Many concerned citizens worked hard and long to get these lands included in the wilderness system. But there is much left to be done. Aldo Leopold wrote in 1949, "Mechanized recreation already has seized nine-tenths of the woods and mountains; a decent respect for minorities should dedicate the other tenth to wilderness." We need to add that additional seven percent Arizona lacks.

There are BLM lands in the southern half of the state, large wildlife refuges such as Cabeza Prieta and Kofa, the popular Grand Canyon National Park, and thousands of acres of other public land which need wilderness designation.

Hikers and backpackers have always been important to the wilderness movement. Their love of wild places fuels conservation efforts. They know the areas which should be protected—and why. They spend long hours learning about their favorite areas: mapping boundaries, resolving conflicts of interest, and working with federal agency personnel. Some of them educate and entertain the public with beautiful slide shows and exciting stories of their adventures. And when it comes down to the nitty gritty, they lobby for "their" wilderness by writing letters to and meeting with their elected officials. If an area is fortunate enough to obtain wilderness designation, then hikers make sure that it is managed in accordance with the wilderness ethic.

I invite you to visit a piece of wild Arizona. You will discover many things about yourself as well as the natural world. And I hope you will help us preserve and protect this valuable resource.—*Dawson Henderson* □

(Dawson Henderson is a coordinator for the Arizona Wilderness Coalition, a non-profit organization working on wilderness and public lands issues in Arizona. They need your support, financially and by lobbying for additional wilderness areas. Please write the Arizona Wilderness Coalition, 2515 E. Thomas Road, Box 16-673, Phoenix, AZ 85016.)

RESOURCES

LOCAL HIKING CLUBS AND CONSERVATION ORGANIZATIONS

Arizona Mountaineering Club, P.O. Box 1695, Phoenix, AZ 85001 (602) 256-0052

Arizona Nature Conservancy, 30 North Tucson Blvd, Tucson, AZ 85716 (602) 327-4478

Arizona Wilderness Coalition, 2515 E. Thomas Road, Box 16-673, Phoenix, AZ 85016

Arizona Wildlife Federation, Rt. 3, Box 50, Flagstaff, AZ 86002

Earth First!, P.O. Box 5871, Tucson, AZ 85703 (602) 622-1371

Maricopa Audubon Society, 4619 East Arcadia Lane, Phoenix, AZ 85018 (602) 959-0052

National Parks & Conservation Association, P.O. Box 67, Cottonwood, AZ 86326 (602) 634-5758

Sierra Club, Grand Canyon Chapter, 5121 N. 13th Avenue, Phoenix, AZ 85013 (602) 279-9427

Tucson Audubon Society, 30-A North Tucson Blvd, Tucson AZ 85716 (602) 749-9808

FEDERAL AND STATE AGENCIES

Bureau of Land Management

Arizona State Office, 2400 Valley Bank Center, Phoenix, AZ 85073 (602) 241-5501

Arizona Strip District Office, 196 East Tabernacle St., George, UT 84770 (801) 673-3545

Phoenix District Office, 2015 West Deer Valley Road, Phoenix, AZ 85027 (602) 863-4464

Safford District Office, 2015 West Deer Valley Road, Phoenix, AZ 85027 (602) 428-4040

Yuma District Office, P.O. Box 5680, 2450 Fourth Avenue, Yuma, AZ 85365 (602) 726-6300

National Park Service

Canyon de Chelly National Monument, Box 588 Chinle, AZ 86503 (602) 674-5436

Chiricahua National Monument Dos Cabezas, Star Route Box 6500, Willcox, AZ 85643 (602) 824-3560

Grand Canyon National Park, P.O. Box 129, Grand Canyon, AZ 86023 (602) 638-2474

Navajo National Monument, HC 63 Box 3, Tonalea, AZ 86044 (602) 672-2366/2367

Organ Pipe Cactus National Monument, P.O. Box 38, Ajo, AZ 85321

Rainbow Bridge National Monument, P.O. Box 1507, Page, AZ 86040 (602) 645-2471

Saguaro National Monument, Old Spanish Trail Route 8, Box 695, Tucson, AZ 85730 (602) 298-2036

National wildlife refuges

Kofa National Wildlife Refuge, P.O. Box 1032, Yuma, AZ 85364

Tribal governments

White Mountain Apache Enterprise Fort Apache Indian Reservation, P.O. Box 218, Whiteriver, AZ 85941 (602) 338-4385

Havasupai Indian Reservation, Havasupai Tourist Enterprise, Supai, AZ 86435 (602) 448-2121

Navajo Indian Reservation, Recreation Resource Department, P.O. Box 308, Window Rock, AZ 86515 (602) 871-6447

United States Forest Service

Apache-Sitgreaves National Forest, P.O. Box 640, Springerville, AZ 85938 (602) 333-4301

Alpine Ranger District, P.O. Box 469, Alpine, AZ 85920 (602) 339-4384

Clifton Ranger District, Box 698, Clifton, AZ 85533 (602) 865-2432

Chevelon Ranger District, 1520 W. 3rd Street, Winslow, AZ 86047 (602) 289-3381

Heber Ranger District, P.O. Box 168, Overgaard, AZ 85933 (602) 535-4481

Lakeside Ranger District, P.O. Box 488, Lakeside, AZ 85929 (602) 368-5111

Springerville Ranger District, P.O. Box 640, Springerville, AZ 86938 (602) 333-4372

Coconino National Forest, 2323 E. Greenlaw Lane, Flagstaff, AZ 86001 (602) 527-7400

Beaver Creek Ranger District, Rimrock, AZ 86335 (602) 567-4501

Blue Ridge Ranger District, Happy Jack, AZ 86024 (602) 477-2255

Elden Ranger District, 2519 E. 7th Avenue, Flagstaff, AZ 86001 (602) 527-7470

Flagstaff Ranger District, 1100 N. Beaver Street, Flagstaff, AZ 86001 (602) 527-7450

Long Valley Ranger District, P.O. Box 68, Happy Jack, AZ 86024 (602) 774-7289

Mormon Lake Ranger District, 4825 S. Lake Mary Road, Flagstaff, AZ 86001 (602) 527-7474

Sedona Ranger District, P.O. Box 300, Sedona, AZ 86336 (602) 282-4119

Coronado National Forest, Federal Building 301 West Congress Tucson, AZ 85701 (602) 629-6483

Douglas Ranger District, Rt. 1, Box 228R, Leslie Canyon Road, Douglas, AZ 85607 (602) 364-3468

Nogales Ranger District, 2480 Tucson-Nogales Hwy., Nogales, AZ 85621 (602) 281-2296

Safford Ranger District, P.O. Box 709, Safford, AZ 85546 (602) 428-4150

Santa Catalina Ranger District, Rt. 15, Box 277F, Tucson, AZ 85715 (602) 629-5113

Sierra Vista Ranger District, R.R. 2, Box 1150, Sierra Vista, AZ 85635 (602) 458-0530

Kaibab National Forest, 800 S. 6th Street, Williams, AZ 86046 (602) 635-2681

Chalender Ranger District, 502 W. Bill Williams Ave., Williams, AZ 86046 (602) 635-2676

North Kaibab Ranger District, P.O. Box 248, Fredonia, AZ 86022 (602) 643-5895

Tusayan Ranger District, P.O. Box 3088, Tusayan, AZ 86023 (602) 638-2443

Williams Ranger District, Rt. 1, Box 142, Williams, AZ 86046 (602) 635-2633

Prescott National Forest, 344 South Cortez Street, P.O. Box 2549, Prescott, AZ 86301 (602) 445-1762

Bradshaw Ranger District RFD 7, Box 3451, Prescott, AZ 86301 (602) 445-7253

Chino Valley Ranger District P.O. Box 285, Chino Valley, AZ 86323 (602) 636-2302

Verde Ranger District HC 62, Box 1100 Camp Verde, AZ 86322 (602) 567-4121

Tonto National Forest, 102 South 28th Street, P.O. Box 29070, Phoenix, AZ 85038 (602) 261-3205

Cave Creek Ranger District, P.O. Box 768, Carefree, AZ 85377 (602) 488-3441

Globe Ranger District, Rt. 1, Box 33 Globe, AZ 85501 (602) 425-7189

Mesa Ranger District, P.O. Drawer A, 26 N. MacDonald, Mesa, AZ 85201 (602) 261-6446

Payson Ranger District, P.O. Box 100 Payson, AZ 85541 (602) 474-2269

Pleasant Valley Ranger District, P.O. Box 268 Young, AZ 85554 (602) 462-3311

Tonto Basin Ranger District, P.O. Box 647, Roosevelt, AZ 85545 (602) 467-2236

State offices

Arizona State Parks, 1688 West Adams Street, Phoenix, AZ 85

FURTHER READING

Aitchison, Stewart. *Oak Creek Canyon and the Red Rock Country Of Arizona: A Natural History and Trail Guide.* Stillwater Canyon Press: Flagstaff, Arizona, 1978.

Aitchison, Stewart. *A Naturalist's Guide to Hiking the Grand Canyon.* Prentice-Hall: Englewood Cliffs, New Jersey, 1985.

Annerino, John. *Hiking the Grand Canyon.* Sierra Club Books: San Francisco, 1986.

Bowman, Eldon. *A Guide to the General Crook Trail.* Museum of Northern Arizona Press: Flagstaff, Arizona, 1978.

Bunker, Gerald. *Arizona's Northland Trails.* La Siesta Press: Glendale, California, 1972.

Butchart, Harvey. *Grand Canyon Treks.* La Siesta Press: Glendale, California, 1970.

Butchart, Harvey. *Grand Canyon Treks II.* La Siesta Press: Glendale, California, 1975.

Butchart, Harvey. *Grand Canyon Treks III.* La Siesta Press: Glendale, California, 1984.

Fletcher, Colin. *The Complete Walker III.* A.A. Knopf: New York, 1984.

Ganci, Dave. *Hiking the Southwest: A Sierra Club Totebook.* Sierra Club Books: San Francisco, 1983.

Heylmun, Edgar. *Guide to the Santa Catalina Mountains of Arizona.* Treasure Chest Publications: Tucson, Arizona, 1979.

Mazel, David. *Arizona Trails.* Wilderness Press: Berkeley, California, 1981.

Morris, Larry. *Hiking the Grand Canyon and Havasupai.* AZTEK Corp.: Tucson, Arizona, 1981.

Mitchell, James. *Fifty Hikes in Arizona.* Gem Guides Book Co.: Pico Rivera, California, 1985.

Nelson, Dick, and Sharon Nelson. *Hiker's Guide to the Superstition Mountains.* Tecolote Press: Glenwood, New Mexico, 1978.

Sheridan, Michael. *Superstition Wilderness Guidebook.* Sheridan Press: Phoenix, Arizona, 1971.

Thybony, Scott. *A Guide to Hiking the Inner Canyon.* Grand Canyon Natural History Association: Grand Canyon, Arizona, 1980.

Wilkerson, James. *Medicine for Mountaineering.* The Mountaineers: Seattle, Washington, 1985.

FINDING MAPS

Arizona national forest and wilderness maps can be obtained from the United States Forest Service regional office at 517 Gold Avenue SW, Albuquerque, NM 87102. Local backpacking specialty shops often stock Forest Service maps.

Bureau of Land Management planimetric maps are similiar to Forest Service maps but cover large areas of public land not included within national parkor national forest boundaries. These maps are available from the United States Geological Survey.

Topographic maps published by the United States Geological Survey (NOT the U.S. Coast and Geodetic Survey) now cover nearly all of Arizona with varying degrees of accuracy and detail. Topos and state map indexes are available directly from the Survey at U.S. Geological Survey, Western Distribution Branch, Box 25286, Denver Federal Center, Denver, CO 80225. These maps are also available from many specialty backpacking shops as well as some general sporting goods stores and engineering supplies.

Getting it all together. A typical assortment of gear for an Arizona backpack trip. Bruce Grubbs

THE HIKER'S CHECKLIST

The following checklist certainly contains more items than any one hiker is likely to need; however, you may find it a useful reference in making sure that you have not forgotten anything essential. Remember to always have plenty of water and warm clothing. It is a good idea to have extra water in your vehicle, too.

Clothing

Shirt
Pants
Underwear
  (extras)
Windshirt
Vest
Belt and/or
  suspenders
Jacket or parka
Turtleneck
Poncho or rain suit
Gloves or mittens
Hat for sun
  and/or cold
  Bandana
Walking shorts
Sweater
Swimming suit

Footwear

Boots
Socks
Boot wax
Moccasins or
  running shoes

Bedroom

Tent Poles
Tent stakes
Cord/guy lines
Fly
Ground cloth
Sleeping bag
Sleeping pad or air mattress

Hauling

Backpack
Day or fanny pack

Cooking

Matches (extra)
Matches (waterproof)
Waterproof match case
Stove
Fuel bottles (filled)

Funnel Pad for stove
Cleaning wire for stove
Cleaning pad for pans
Fire starter
Cook kit
Pot gripper
Spatula
Cup
Bowl/plate
Utensils
Dish rag
Dish towel
Plastic bottle and/or
  canteen

Food and drink

Cereal
Bread
Crackers
Cheese
Margarine
Powdered soups
Salt/pepper
Main course meals
Snacks
Hot chocolate
Tea
Powdered milk
Drink mixes

Photography

Camera
  Film (extras)
Extra lenses
Filters
Close-up attachments
Tripod
Lens brush/paper
Light meter
Flash equipment

Miscellaneous

Fishing gear
Pocket knife
Whetstone
Compass
Topo maps

Other maps
Sunglasses
Flashlight
Batteries (extra)
Bulbs
Candle lantern
First aid kit
Snakebite kit
Survival kit
Repair kit
Sunscreen
Insect repellent
Toilet paper
Space blanket
Binoculars
Nylon cord
Plastic bags
Rubber bands/ties
Whistle
Salt tablets
Emergency fishing gear
Wallet/I.D. cards
  Dimes for phone calls
Ripstop tape
Notebook and pencils
Field guides
Toothpaste
Dental floss
Mirror
Garbage bag
Book
Towel
Safety pins
Scissors
Trowel
Water purification
  system
Car key
Signal flare
Watch
Extra parts for stove,
  pack, and tent
Rubber tubing
  (to suck water out of
  shallow, rain-filled
  potholes)

ACKNOWLEDGMENTS

We wish to thank all of you who made this book a reality. Special thanks go out to the hikers who over the years have freely given of their time and knowledge to allow us to explore the wonderful state of Arizona.

It was a tremendous help to receive trail descriptions from Tom Bean, Steve Gustafson, Sid Hirsh, Steve Knox, Rudi Lambrechtse, Ken Mahoney, John Nelson, Gary Russell, and Bill Williams. Legendary Grand Canyon hiker Harvey Butchart generously loaned us his monumental collection of hiking notes.

Thanks, too, to Dale Shewalter for his description of the Arizona Trail, Dawson Henderson of the Arizona Wilderness Coalition for his essay, and Governor Bruce Babbitt, Arizona's most famous hiker, for writing the preface.

Many individuals with the Bureau of Land Management, National Park Service, and United States Forest Service gave generously of their time and knowledge and we appreciate it.

Last but certainly not least, we thank Bill Schneider, Russell Hill, Linda McCray, and all the fine folks at Falcon Press for transforming our rough notes into a real guide book.—*Stewart Aitchison and Bruce Grubbs*

THE AUTHORS

Stewart Aitchison is a guide for Special Expeditions, Inc. and escorts travelers on natural history trips around the greater Southwest. He has written numerous scientific and popular articles as well as four previous books: *Oak Creek Canyon and the Red Rock of Arizona, A Naturalist's San Juan River Guide, A Naturalist's Guide to Hiking the Grand Canyon,* and *Utah Wildlands.* When not out exploring, he lives in Flagstaff, Arizona with his wife, Ann, and two cats.

Bruce Grubbs has been actively backpacking, cross-country skiing, and climbing in the Southwest for twenty years. He has participated in a number of first ascents of difficult buttes and peaks in the Grand Canyon, as well as a number of very long hiking trips. He has extensively explored much of Arizona's wilderness areas, as well as many areas not officially protected. He is currently attending Cochise College in southeast Arizona.